A Phenomenology of Landscape
Places, Paths and Monuments

Christopher Tilley

BERG

Oxford/Providence, USA

First published in 1994 by
Berg Publishers
Editorial offices:
150 Cowley Road, Oxford, OX4 1JJ, UK
221 Waterman Road, Providence, RI 02906, USA

Library of Congress Cataloging-in-Publication Data
A catalogue record for this book is available from the British
Library.

British Library Cataloguing in Publication Data
A catalogue record for this book is available from the British
Library.

ISBN 0 85496 919 5 (Cloth)
     1 85973 076 0 (Paper)

A Phenomenology of Landscape

EXPLORATIONS IN ANTHROPOLOGY
A University College London Series

Series Editors: Barbara Bender, John Gledhill and Bruce Kapferer

Joan Bestard-Camps, *What's in a Relative? Household and Family in Formentera*

Henk Driessen, *On the Spanish-Moroccan Frontier: A Study in Ritual, Power and Ethnicity*

Alfred Gell, *The Anthropology of Time: Cultural Construction of Temporal Maps and Images*

Tim Ingold, David Riches and James Woodburn (eds), *Hunters and Gatherers*

  Volume 1. *History, Evolution and Social Change*
  Volume 2. *Property, Power and Ideology*

Bruce Kapferer, *A Celebration of Demons* (2nd edn.)

Guy Lanoue, *Brothers: The Politics of Violence among the Sekani of Northern British Columbia*

Jadran Mimica, *Intimations of Infinity: The Mythopoeia of the Iqwaye Counting System and Number*

Barry Morris, *Domesticating Resistance: The Dhan-Gadi Aborigines and the Australian State*

Thomas C. Paterson, *The Inca Empire: The Formation and Disintegration of a Pre-Capitalist State*

Max and Eleanor Rimoldi, *Hahalis and the Labour of Love: A Social Movement on Buka Island*

Pnina Werbner, *The Migration Process: Capital, Gifts and Offerings among Pakistanis in Britain*

Joel S. Kahn, *Constituting the Minangkabau: Peasants, Culture, and Modernity in Colonial Indonesia*

Gisli Polsson, *Beyond Boundaries: Understanding, Translation and Anthropological Discourse*

Stephen Nugent, *Amazonian Caboclo Society*

Barbara Bender, *Landscape: Politics and Perspectives*

Christopher Tilley (ed.), *Interpretative Archaeology*

Ernest S. Burch, Jr. and Linda J. Ellanna, *Key Issues in Hunter-Gatherer Research*

Daniel Miller, *Modernity – An Ethnographic Approach: Dualism and Mass Consumption in Trinidad*

Robert Pool, *Dialogue and the Interpretation of Illness: Conversations in a Cameroon Village*

Contents

List of Illustrations

List of Tables

Introduction

This book, in many ways, is an exercise in a 'blurred genre', involving insights acquired through a reading of works of a phenomenological approach in philosophy, cultural anthropology, and human geography and recent interpretative work in archaeology. It is not intended to 'represent' any of these fields, or individual positions taken within them, but rather aims to set elements of them to work pragmatically in a consideration of prehistoric landscapes.

The book is divided into two Parts. In the first, Chapter 1 sets out a general theoretical perspective on the significance of spaces, places and landscapes in small-scale, non-Western societies. Chapter 2 considers issues of landscape use and perception in relation to hunter–gatherers and subsistence cultivators from a consideration of ethnographic literature. The second Part of the book is an empirical exercise in attempting to develop a framework with which to understand long-term relationships between people and features of the landscape. Chapters 3, 4 and 5 discuss the development of archaeological landscapes from the Mesolithic to the Neolithic. The key question addressed is deceptively simple: why were particular locations chosen for habitation and the erection of monuments as opposed to others? It is of central importance for the interpretative reconstruction of prehistoric lifeworlds. The standard approach to such a question within the archaeological literature has concentrated on factors of the environment such as relief, climate, soils, water supply and the seasonal availability of exploitable resources. These have been related to factors such as demographic patterns, technologies, transhumance systems, territoriality, and control over exchange networks and forms of social organization facilitating environmental exploitation as a means of adaptation (e.g. Binford 1978, 1980; Hodder and Orton 1976; Jarman, Bailey and Jarman 1982; Webley 1976; Roese 1982). The location of sites thus becomes explained as a result of a mix of 'rational' decision-making

1

processes involving some or all of these factors. The statistical correlations and functional interdependencies arrived at are the function of a contemporary myth-making in which an exclusively modernist Western logic has simply become superimposed on the past. In the process how people may have perceived the landscape in which they lived is either regarded as irrevocably lost, or irrelevant, or both. Cultural meanings are only unimportant for those who choose to make them so. Here I wish to stress two features in particular – the symbolics of landscape perception and the role of social memory in choice of site location. In so doing I do not wish to set up a polar divide between a supposed economic rationality and a cultural or symbolic logic but rather to suggest that each helps to constitute the other. People do not, of course, deliberately occupy inhospitable habitats or those with few resources by virtue of some slavish accommodation to a symbolic scheme; but the places that they do occupy take on, through time, particular sets of meanings and connotations which are at least partially interpretable from archaeological evidence and appear to be too important to be ignored.

Three study areas provide the substantive data-base for the discussion: Pembrokeshire in south-west Wales, the Black Mountains area of south-east Wales, and Cranborne Chase in Dorset. These comprise one coastal and two inland regions of markedly different topography. All three major classes of Neolithic monuments are represented in these regions: a western tradition involving the construction of portal dolmens and chambered cairns in Pembrokeshire; Cotswold–Severn type chambered long cairns in the Black Mountains; and earthen long barrows covering timber or turf mortuary houses in Cranborne Chase. All three areas have Mesolithic sites represented, in the main, by surface flint scatters.

The regions considered are all, in their different ways, distinctive natural landscapes with marked differences in local relief highlighting the relationship between sites and their settings, which, I will argue, is of fundamental importance. The primary concern in the book is the location of Mesolithic sites and Neolithic cairns and mounds and their internal chambers in relation to dominant features in the surrounding landscape – rivers, the coast, spurs, escarpment edges, rock outcrops and ridges. This is a type of analysis that has hardly been explored in any detail previously. Attention has tended to focus either on the sites themselves, in the form of ground plans and excavation reports, or at the much broader spatial scale of the overall distribution map or the presumed 'site catchment territory', where locations become simply dots in a two-dimensional space situated in relation to drainage patterns, perhaps soil types, and a choice of contour intervals. The archaeologist appears as a mole whose head hardly rises above the site itself to consider wider sets of relationships between it and the environment in which it is situated or, alternatively, surveys everything on the distribution map as if from an aircraft. This is even reflected in the form of published photographs in books and journals, which almost always tend to concentrate on the sites themselves to the exclusion of their surroundings. The research discussed in this paper might be described as 'middle-range' in so far as it is aimed at filling a gap between the site plan and the distribution map.

I am grateful to George Nash for help in surveying the Neolithic monuments in Wales, Julian Thomas for constructive comments on an early draft of parts of the manuscript and Stuart Laidlaw for developing and printing the photographs at short notice. Barbara Bender, Mark Edmonds and Mike Rowlands were kind enough to read through a second draft of the entire manuscript and I thank them for their constructive criticisms and comments, to which I have tried to respond in the published version.

Christopher Tilley
London, 1994

Part I
Landscape – Theoretical and Contemporary Perspectives

Chapter 1

Space, Place, Landscape and Perception: Phenomenological Perspectives

Introduction: Spatial Science to Humanized Space

During the past thirty years a striking series of parallels and convergences have taken place in human geography and archaeology. Until the 1960s both disciplines were largely empiricist in outlook and concerned with distinctiveness and difference in various ways. Human geography was dominated by the study of regions at various spatial scales – North America, Africa, Asia, regions of Britain or Canada, etc., treated in a holistic manner. The resulting syntheses tended to start by discussing geology, climate and soils and ended by considering such matters as welfare provision and political systems. This was the geographical equivalent of the anthropological monograph in which 'everything' was brought together into a whole. In a similar way archaeology was concerned with space-time systematics and the ordering of artefacts and other evidence into cultural units within a delimited territorial area with a putative ethnic significance.

The 'revolutions' of the 'new' geography and the 'new' archaeology consigned such a perspective to an unenlightened Dark Age of superstition and misunderstanding. Replacing it all was the white heat of positivism coupled with functionalism, in which a notion of geography as spatial science and archaeology as a science of the past were borne. The history of and the subsequent disillusionment with this approach are well known, and there is no need to rehearse them here in any detail.

As a component of the retheorization of human geography from the 1970s onwards and in archaeology during the 1980s the usefulness of a 'scientific' conception of space abstracted from human affairs has systematically been called into question (e.g. Harvey 1973; Relph 1976; Gregory 1978; Gregory and Urry 1985;

Soja 1989; Hodder 1982a,b, 1986, 1987, 1992; Miller and Tilley 1984; Shanks and Tilley 1987a,b,1989; Bender 1992, 1993; Tilley 1994). The major differences between a 'scientific' or abstract and a 'humanized' or meaning-laden space can be summarized as follows:

container	medium
decentred	centred
geometry	context
surfaces	densities
universal	specific
objective	subjective
substantial	relational
totalized	detotalized
external	internal
system	strategy
neutral	empowered
coherence	contradiction
atemporal	temporal
ABSTRACT SPACE	HUMAN SPACE

materialist, rational   idealist, irrational

The list might be considerably extended, or the couplets abbreviated, since they clearly overlap. I have added a cross-over between the lists of terms at the bottom in order to indicate that the approach which has usually been claimed as the hallmark of an objective, rational and materialist approach to space (the left-hand column) now appears, in view of the weight of contemporary arguments, as a form of irrational idealism and vice versa.

It is from the general perspective of the terms listed in the right-hand column that this book both takes its starting-point and attempts to develop in relation to a consideration of landscape. While not wishing to dwell too much here on the antagonistic history of past debates it seems necessary to explain and unpack the columns of oppositions as a background to the rest of the book.

New geography and new archaeology considered space as an abstract dimension or container in which human activities and events took place. The implication of this perspective was that activity and event and space were conceptually and physically separate from each other and only contingently related. Such a view of space decentred it from agency and meaning. It was something that could be objectively measured in terms of an abstracted geometry of scale. Space was quite literally a nothingness, a simple surface for action, lacking depth. This space was universal, everywhere and anywhere the same, and had cross-cultural impact on people and society. People had to move across this space, and movement through it, for example, created 'friction' limiting human potentialities. The effects of distance and the varying potentialities of site locations could be objectively specified on one and the same spatial scale of measurement. Space as container, surface and volume was substantial inasmuch as it existed in itself and for itself, external to and indifferent to human affairs. The neutrality of this space resulted in its being divorced from any consideration of structures of power and domination. A space divorced from humanity and society provided a coherent and unitary backdrop for any analysis, since it was always the same. The space of the palaeolithic was the same as the space of late capitalism, that of Vancouver identical to that of Canberra. As a dimension in which human action took place it was directly equivalent to and separate from time, the second primary and abstracted scale according to which societal change could be documented and 'measured'.

The attraction of this perspective was, no doubt, its purity and simplicity and the potential it offered for comparative studies of the organization of artefacts, sites, populations, and flows of information and exchange across regions and landscapes. All could be objectively plotted on maps, distances measured and expressed according to the same rigorous and quantitative scale.

Quantification, mathematization and computer modelling seemingly offered unlimited potential for unravelling the spatial fix of human affairs. Burning issues of the day in geography and archaeology became what sampling fractions to use, how to construct appropriate boundaries for a nearest-neighbour analysis, what were the best statistics to use and the development of alternative methodologies for measuring and describing the abstract geometry of space. Lurking beneath the distribution of the dots on a map was a spatial process and causality to be discovered.

The linkages between new geography and new archaeology were quite explicit. Clarke's *Models in Archaeology* (1972) was itself modelled on Chorley and Haggett's *Models in Geography* (1967), Harvey's *Explanation in Geography* (1969) found its archaeological counterpart in *Explanation in Archaeology* (Watson *et al.* 1971). Clarke (1972) identified a 'geographical paradigm' to archaeological research which was simply the extension of the spatial methodology of the new geography to archaeological evidence, while Renfrew (1969) predicted that the texts of new geographers would provide source books in methods for future generations of archaeologists.

Accordingly 'new' geography was systematically used to provide the basis for a mathematical spatial archaeology (Hodder and Orton 1976; Clarke 1977). The traditional archaeological distribution map of sites and artefacts now became clothed with thiessen polygons, site catchments, regression lines, trend surfaces and gravity models, all reflecting in various ways the 'friction' and impact of space on human affairs (for reviews see Goudie 1987; Wagstaff 1987a).

The alternative view starts from regarding space as a medium rather than a container for action, something that is involved in action and cannot be divorced from it. As such, space does not and cannot exist apart from the events and activities within which it is implicated. Space is socially produced, and different societies, groups and individuals act out their lives in different spaces. Space in itself no longer becomes a meaningful term. There is no space, only spaces. These spaces, as social productions, are always centred in relation to human agency and are amenable to reproduction or change because their constitution takes place as part of the day-to-day *praxis* or practical activity of individuals and groups in the world. They are meaningfully constituted in relation to human agency and activity. A humanized space forms both the medium and outcome of action, both constraining and enabling it. A centred and meaningful space involves specific sets of linkages between the physical space of the non-humanly created world, somatic states of the body, the mental space of cognition and representation and the space of movement, encounter and interaction between persons and between persons and the human and non-human environment. Socially produced space combines the cognitive, the physical and the emotional into something that may be reproduced but is always open to transformation and change. A social space, rather than being uniform and forever the same, is constituted by differential densities of human experience, attachment and involvement. It is above all contextually constituted, providing particular settings for involvement and the creation of meanings. The specificity of place is an essential element in understanding its significance. It follows that the meanings of space always involve a subjective dimension and cannot be understood apart from the symbolically constructed lifeworlds of social actors. Space has no substantial essence in itself, but only has a relational significance, created through relations between peoples and places. Space becomes detotalized by virtue of its relational construction and because, being differentially understood and produced by different individuals, collectivities and societies, it can have no universal essence. What space is depends on who is experiencing it and how. Spatial experience is not innocent and neutral, but invested with power relating to age, gender, social position and relationships with others. Because space is differentially understood and experienced it forms a contradictory and conflict-ridden medium through which individuals act and are acted upon. The experience of space is always shot through with temporalities, as spaces are always created, reproduced and transformed in relation to previously constructed spaces provided and established from the past. Spaces are intimately related to the formation of biographies and social relationships.

Such a notion of space is undoubtedly complex. There is and can be no clear-cut methodology arising from it to provide a concise guide to empirical research. The approach requires, rather, a continuous dialectic between ideas and empirical data. From this perspective, the intimate connection of space with the social, with the formation of biographies, with action, event, power, context and subjectivity, materializes or concretizes its specificity and impact in the social world. We move from the irrational abstracted idealism of a geometrical universal space to an ontological grounding of space in the differential structuring of human experience and action in the world: a perspective which now requires examination in more detail.

A Phenomenological Perspective

The key issue in any phenomenological approach is the manner in which people experience and understand the world.

Phenomenology involves the understanding and description of things as they are experienced by a subject. It is about the relationship between Being and Being-in-the-world. Being-in-the-world resides in a process of objectification in which people objectify the world by setting themselves apart from it. This results in the creation of a gap, a distance in space. To be human is both to create this distance between the self and that which is beyond and to attempt to bridge this distance through a variety of means – through perception (seeing, hearing, touching), bodily actions and movements, and intentionality, emotion and awareness residing in systems of belief and decision-making, remembrance and evaluation.

Let us think for a while of a farmhouse in the Black Forest, which was built some two hundred years ago by the dwelling of peasants. Here the self-sufficiency of the power to let earth and heaven, divinities and mortals enter in *simple oneness* into things, ordered the house. It placed the farm on the wind-sheltered mountain slope looking south, among the meadows close to the spring. It gave it the wide overhanging shingle roof whose proper slope bears up under the burden of snow, and which, reaching deep down, shields the chambers against the storms of the long winter nights. It did not forget the altar corner behind the community table; it made room in its chamber for the hallowed places of childbed and the 'tree of the dead' – for that is what they call a coffin there: the *Totenbaum* – and in this way it is designed for the different generations under one roof the character of their journey through time. A craft which, itself sprung from dwelling, still uses its tools and frames as things, built the farmhouse (Heidegger 1972: 338).

The fact is that if we want to describe it, we must say that my experience breaks forth into things and transcends itself in them, because it always comes into being within the framework of a certain setting in relation to the world which is the definition of my body ... Any perception of a thing, a shape or a size as real, any perceptual constancy refers back to the positing of a world and of a system of experience in which my body is inescapably linked with phenomena. But the system of experience is not arrayed before me as if I were God, it is lived by me from a certain point of view; I am not the spectator, I am involved, and it is my involvement in a point of view which makes possible both the finiteness of my perception and its opening out upon the complete world as a horizon of every perception (Merleau-Ponty 1962: 303–4).

I have let Heidegger and Merleau-Ponty set the scene. From rather different phenomenological perspectives, they have both stressed important ontological characteristics of the relationship between inhabited space and social Being-in-the-world. For Heidegger 'spaces receive their essential being from locations and not from "space"' (1972: 332). A mathematical 'space' of measurement contains no spaces, places or locations, for it is not humanized. Spaces open up by virtue of the *dwelling* of humanity or the *staying with things* that cannot be separated: the earth, the sky and the constellations, the divinities, birth and death. Space is that something for which room is made. Building produces things as locations and building and thinking both belong to dwelling. Heidegger proposes a *topological* model for thinking about the relationship between people and the landscape as a matter of the 'thereness' of the self-disclosure of Being in and of the world. Cognition is not opposed to reality, but is wholly given over in the total social fact of dwelling, serving to link place, praxis, cosmology and nurture.

If 'dwelling', in Heideggerian terms, forms a primordial part of that which it is to be human, this necessarily requires a consideration of the body as the privileged vantage point from which the world is apprehended. The kinetic activities of human beings orientate apprehension of the landscape and create it as human. Space is existential, and existence is spatial in that it opens onto an 'outside', a series of reference points (Merleau-Ponty 1962: 293). Merleau-Ponty, like Heidegger, attempts to chart a middle course between an empiricist objectivism and a cognitive idealism. With empiricist objectivism, the perception of space and the environment, like everything else, is an event in nature. Perception is the causal physical or chemical action of a thing on an organ which sensation registers. Everything takes place in a world of pure objectivity, and there is no *subject* who perceives. Conversely, a cognitive idealism posits an absolute subjectivity involving a transcendental Ego who is the subject of experience. In a relation of pure interiority the objective world exists only in relation to a consciousness which projects that world before itself. For Merleau-Ponty the problem of both of these positions is that they systematically evade the problem of the phenomenon of perception, empiricism because it makes an object of the subject, cognitive idealism because it reduces the perception of the object to an operation of thought (ibid.: 39). Merleau-Ponty argues that the human body provides the fundamental mediation point between thought and the world. The world and the subject reflect and flow into each other through the body that provides the living bond with the world. Notions of 'object' and 'subject', 'nature' and 'consciousness' are dialectically related moments of a totality which is constituted through the Being of the body in the world. The body constitutes a way of relating to, perceiving and understanding the world. It is the manner in which a subjective attitude comes to both know and express itself. Perceptual consciousness is not just a matter of thought about the world, but stems from bodily presence and bodily orientation in relation to it, bodily *awareness*: 'far from my body's being for me no more than a fragment of space, there would be no space at all for me if I had no body' (ibid.: 102).

While 'dwelling' occurs in different varieties and textures of humanly created space, this social existence is, of course, rooted in natural and non-humanly created environments. The concept of dwelling, with its fourfold ontological implications as pointed out by Heidegger, the human body as a focus for the perception of a humanized world, and the groundedness of social Being in that which is not humanly created constitute the fundamental presuppositions for beginning to think about the relationship between people and landscape in a fresh manner. Subjectivity and objectivity connect in a dialectic producing a *place* for *Being* in which the topography and physiography of the land and thought remain distinct but play into each other as an 'intelligible landscape', a spatialization of Being, which I will now examine in a less abstract manner.

Space and Place

If space allows movement, place is pause (Taun 1977: 6).

The relationship between space and place has been discussed and theorized from one particular perspective within a phenomenological 'school' of geographical research (Taun 1974, 1975, 1977; Pickles 1985; Relph 1976; Buttimer and Seamon 1980; Seamon and Mugerauer 1989). The key concern in this approach is the manner in which places *constitute* space as centres of human meaning, their singularity being manifested and expressed in the

day-to-day experiences and consciousness of people within particular lifeworlds. Such an approach starts from an initial presup-
position claiming the wholeness and indivisibility of a human
experience of place, and that meaning, defined in terms of structures of intentionality, is central to any understanding of place.
Knowledge of place stems from human experiences, feeling and
thought. Space is a far more abstract construct than place. It provides a situational context for places, but derives its meanings
from particular places (Relph 1976: 8). Without places there can
be no spaces, and the former have primary ontological significance as centres of bodily activity, human significance and emotional attachment. The meaning of place is grounded in
existential or lived consciousness of it. It follows that the limits of
place are grounded in the limits of human consciousness. Places
are as diffuse and differentiated as the range of identities and significances accorded to them. People are immersed in a world of
places which the geographical imagination aims to understand
and recover – places as contexts for human experience, constructed in movement, memory, encounter and association. There may
be a strong affection for place (topophilia) or aversion (topopho-
bia), but places are always far more than points or locations,
because they have distinctive meanings and values for persons.
Personal and cultural identity is bound up with place; a topo-
analysis is one exploring the creation of self-identity through
place. Geographical experience begins in places, reaches out to
others through spaces, and creates landscapes or regions for
human existence.

Attempts have been made in the literature to generalize the
specificity of place by erecting typologies of particular kinds of
spaces through which the identities of place are constructed.
Such classifications can only act as heuristic devices, since it can
be argued that places, by their very nature, contain sedimented
meanings which resist such boxing and bracketing of their
natures and significance. The following forms of space might be
identified:

1. Somatic space
2. Perceptual space
3. Existential space
4. Architectural space
5. Cognitive space

Somatic space is a space of habitual and unselfconscious action. It is the space of sensory experience and bodily movement. An understanding of this space takes as its starting-point the upright human body looking out on the world. Space opens out before the body and is differentiable in terms of front/back; left/right; vertical/horizontal; top/bottom; within reach/ beyond reach; within hearing/beyond hearing; within sight/ beyond sight; here/there polarities (Relph 1976: 9; Taun 1977: 35–50). The very physicality of the body imposes a schema on space through which it may be experienced and understood. An experience of space is grounded in the body itself; its capacities and potentialities for movement. Through time–space routines of movement a person knows where she or he is in relation to familiar places and objects and 'how to go on' in the world. Lived body-space incorporates not only habituated movement in general but also modes of walking, turning, reaching in performing particular acts: body-ballets (Seamon 1979, 1980).

Perceptual space is the egocentric space perceived and encountered by individuals in their daily practices. The centre of such a space is grounded in individual perception of distances and directions, natural objects and cultural creations. This space is always relative and qualitative. Distance and direction are perceived as near or far, this way or that way, moving along one track or another. A perceptual space is one that links patterns of individual intentionality to bodily movement and perception. It is a space of personality, of encounter and emotional attachment. It is the constructed life-space of the individual, involving feelings and memories giving rise to a sense of awe, emotion, wonder or anguish in spatial encounters. Such a space may as often as not be felt rather than verbalized. It creates personal significances for an individual in his or her bodily routines – places remembered and places of affective importance.

Perceptual space is intricately interlinked with existential space or the lived space as it is constructed in the concrete experiences of individuals socialized within a group. The meanings of existential space transcend the individual and form a grounding for perceptual space rather than being some kind of summation of individualized perception. Existential space is in a constant process of production and reproduction through the movements and activities of members of a group. It is a mobile rather than a passive space for experience. It is experienced and created through life-activity, a sacred, symbolic and mythic space replete with social meanings wrapped around buildings, objects and features of the local topography, providing reference points and planes of emotional orientation for human attachment and involvement. Places in existential space are foci for the production of meaning, intention and purpose of societal significance. Boundaries are of major significance in structuring existential space both in and between places and regions. Boundaries are to do with creating distinctions and marking out social oppositions, mapping social and cultural difference and Otherness. The presence of boundaries, obvious natural prototypes being river courses, mountain chains, or rock outcrops, and the coast, may be of major significance in delimiting territories, the choice of locales and the networking of paths through a landscape.

Architectural space only makes sense in relation to pragmatic, perceptual and existential space, but involves a deliberate attempt to create and bound space, create an inside, an outside, a way around, a channel for movement. Architecture is the deliberate creation of space made tangible, visible and sensible. This is why buildings play a fundamental role in the creation and recreation, production and reproduction of existential space and have profound structuring effects on perceptual space.

Finally, cognitive space provides a basis for reflection and theorization with regard to understanding the others. It is the 'space' of this discussion and analysis.

Space can only exist as a set of relations between things or places. In this sense there is no space that is not relational. Space is created by social relations, natural and cultural objects. It is a production, an achievement, rather than an autonomous reality in which things or people are located or 'found'. Having been constituted by things and places spatial relations affect the way in which they relate. In other words, there is a sociospatial dialectic at work – space is both constituted and constitutive.

Locales, Social Action

Places may, of course, be experienced and conceptualized at any number of spatial levels, from personal space to community space to regional space and so on. Places overlap according to scales of action, interest, movement and concern. Place is an irreducible part of human experience, a person is 'in place' just as much as she or he is 'in culture'. Place is about situatedness in relation to identity and action. In this sense place is context, and there can be no non-contextual definition of context or place. The specificity of space always has to be understood from a particular viewpoint.

In small-scale non-Western societies place, defined as a centre for action, intention and meaningful concern, can be best considered in terms of locales and the wider context in which these locales occur – the cultural and natural landscape. Most significant places are located or positioned in space. Locales are places created and known through common experiences, symbols and meanings. They may be rooms, houses, monuments, meeting-places, camps or settlements. Locales may offer a distinct quality of being inside, or part of, a place. People both live out their lives in place and have a sense of being part of it. Consequently, place is fundamental to the establishment of personal and group identities and the formation of biographies. Place is both 'internal' and 'external' to the human subject, a personally embedded centre of meanings and a physical locus for action. All places thus have metonymic qualities (places and their contents consist of part–whole relations) and differential densities of meanings to their inhabitants according to the events and actions they witness, partake in and remember. A sense of attachment to place is frequently derived from the stability of meanings associated with it.

The naming and identification of particular topographical features, such as sand dunes, bays and inlets, mountain peaks, etc., settlements and sites is crucial for the establishment and maintenance of their identity. Through an act of naming and through the development of human and mythological associations such places become invested with meaning and significance. Place names are of such vital significance because they act so as to transform the sheerly physical and geographical into something that is historically and socially experienced. The bestowing of names creates shared existential space out of a blank environment (Basso 1984: 27; Weiner 1991: 32). By the process of naming places and things they become captured in social discourses and act as mnemonics for the historical actions of individuals and groups. Without a name culturally significant sites would not exist, but only as a raw void, a natural environment. In a fundamental way names create landscapes. An unnamed place on a map is quite literally a blank space. Names may create places of human import; but they do so in relation to the raw material at hand. For example, the vast majority of Western Apache place-names are lengthy and made up of descriptions of the locations to which they refer, for example *tséká tú yahilíí* (water flows downward on top of a series of flat rocks) or 'coarse-textured rocks lie above in a compact cluster' (Basso 1984: 28, 37). Place-names are used in Apache story-telling as situational or contextualizing devices for locating narrative events in physical settings. The description of the setting is accomplished by the use of the place-name itself (see below).

From the perspective of structuration theory Giddens has emphasized the role of locales in processes of social production and reproduction (Giddens 1979, 1981, 1984). Structure considered as a set of rules and resources for action is the medium through which action is produced, both enabling and constraining it. Structure is also a product of action, and is created, reproduced and changed through the meaningful action of agents. Action affects structure by virtue of its temporal and spatial specificity. Time and space are components of action rather than containers for it. Space plays an important part in defining the manner in which social interaction takes place and the significance it has for agents. Locales are settings in which interaction takes place. 'A setting is not just a spatial parameter, and physical environment, in which interaction occurs: it is these elements mobilized as part of the interaction. Features of the setting of interaction, including its spatial and physical aspects ... are routinely drawn upon by social actors in the sustaining of communication' (Giddens 1979: 206). Spatial contingency and difference in this formulation have clear effects on the manner in which agents interrelate, but this needs to be viewed as a dialectic rather than a causal relationship in order to avoid the pitfalls of a spatial fetishism or an environmental determinism (Saunders 1989; Duncan 1989). Actors *draw* on their settings; and the manner in which they do so depends upon the specificity of their relationship to place. In this manner locales, in the most general sense, can be defined as a presencing of potentialities on which actors draw in the daily conduct of their activities.

Giddens extends the usage of the term locale to include large-scale territorial aggregations such as nation states or empires. It thus becomes a nested concept on a sliding spatial scale, in which distinctions between locale, locality, region, etc. become blurred. It is far better to confine the usage of the term to the small-scale and the specific. Locales occur in localities, regions or landscapes. Duncan (1989) seriously questions whether there is anything such as locality which can be meaningfully distinguished from the non-local recounting the quip that regional geographers are 'trying to put boundaries that do not exist around regions that do not matter' (Duncan 1989: 238). But he is writing within the context of the development of a theoretical geography of the modern world system. While we might accept that it is virtually impossible to distinguish distinctive spatial parameters of whatever might be defined as 'locality' within contemporary Britain such a conclusion is anachronistic and unhelpful when transferred to the past. A sense of 'placelessness' referred to by Relph (1976) and others in contemporary society is, in essence, to do with the systematic erosion of locality as meaningful. This discussion inevitably brings us to the politics of space.

The Politics of Space

If space is to be regarded as a medium for action, a resource in which actors draw on in their activity and use for their own purposes, it inevitably becomes value-laden rather than value-free and political rather than neutral. At a high level of generality it is possible to distinguish between essential characteristics of Western and capitalist 'spaces' and non-Western and pre-capitalist 'spaces':

infinitely open	different densities
desanctified	sanctified
control	sensuousness
surveillance/partitioning	ritualized/anthropomorphic
economic	cosmological
'useful' to act	'useful' to think
architectural forms resemble each other in 'disciplinary' space	architecture an embodiment of myth and cosmology

landscape as backdrop to action	landscape as sedimented ritual form
time linear and divorced from space	time constitutive of rhythms of social action in space–time
CAPITALIST/WESTERN SPACE	PRE-CAPITALIST/ NON-WESTERN SPACE

The distinctions made above might be considered dominant trends or 'ideal types', in that it is cleárly not the case that capitalist or Western spaces are devoid of meanings or significances (see for example the studies in Gold and Burgess 1982; Penning-Rosewell and Lowenthal 1986); and pre-capitalist spaces were, of course, 'useful to act', 'economic' places equally subject to exploitation. However, it remains the case that numerous authors, a massive environmental lobby, and a 'green movement' have consistently remarked on the manner in which landscapes, buildings, places and localities in contemporary society seem to have lost, or be in the process of losing, their value and significance. The space created by market forces must, above all, be a useful and rational place. Once stripped of sedimented human meanings, considered to be purely epiphenomenal and irrelevant, the landscape becomes a surface or volume like any other, open for exploitation and everywhere homogeneous in its potential exchange value for any particular project. It becomes desanctified, set apart from people, myth and history, something to be controlled and used.

Foucault (1986) remarks on the manner in which the work of Galileo and others 'opened out' a medieval space of emplacement in which microcosm mirrored macrocosm, the celestial providing a map for the worldly and vice versa. In the new space thus created the division and 'rational' utilization of space comes increasingly to the fore, and in modern Western 'disciplinary' societies (Foucault 1977) the control and distribution of people in space becomes of central concern. The map becomes a means of inquiry, of examination and control – electoral maps, maps of ethnic groups, taxation maps, etc. Discipline can only be effective through the control and structuring of space; and hence it is not surprising that prisons resemble hospitals, which resemble schools, and factories, which resemble prisons (Foucault 1977: 228).

Relph comments that 'the paradox of modern landscapes is that they are dehumanising because they are excessively humanised. There is almost nothing in them that has not been conceived and planned so that it will serve those human needs which can be assessed in terms of efficiency or improved material conditions. But there is almost nothing in them that can happen spontaneously, autonomously or accidentally, or which expresses human emotions and feelings' (Relph 1981: 104). This opposition between a past of supposed 'spontaneity' and 'freedom' and a present of rational calculation and control seems somewhat overdrawn. If the political qualities of a capitalist landscape relate to a dominant cultural construction of a 'useful', disciplinary space of social control, pre-capitalist spaces are no less invested with forms of power, but within a qualitatively different landscape invested with mythological understandings and ritual knowledges intimately linked with bodily routines and practices.

Landscape and the Scape of Praxis

Spaces and places relationally constitute wider contexts for social practices-landscapes. Anthropologists and archaeologists have been interested for a long time in the relationships between people and the landscape, conceived rather narrowly as 'environmental milieu', but for the most part research has tended to focus on functional and supposedly adaptive parameters of these relationships, with matters such as population levels, resource 'ceilings' and environmental constraints. The vast majority of studies of hunter–fisher–gatherers have tended to concentrate rather narrowly on issues such as the ranges of food resources exploited, food-getting technologies, seasonality and scheduling in relation to settlement size, location and group composition, and degree of mobility. In this approach myths, cosmologies and symbolism are largely deemed irrelevant to what is really going on. What people *think* about the environment has little or no affect on the practical exigencies of having to live in it. On the other hand, there exists a vast body of literature concerned with the analysis of ritual performance and cosmological and social structures in which the environment is equally irrelevant, a mere backdrop to the unconstrained ramifications of the human mind.

A naturalistic view of landscape as a neutral backdrop to activity is clearly of recent origin in thought, an irrelevance in considering pre-capitalist landscapes, and a hindrance in their conceptualization. It is also a highly ideological construct which requires deconstruction even in the context of capitalist landscapes. A culturalist view of landscape as a highly specific, symbolic and cognitive ordering of space offers far more potential in understanding but, as Ingold argues (Ingold 1992, 1993), encloses humanity into a series of separate cultural worlds constituted as structured sets of shared representations divorced from 'nature' or the physical world. This external world provides a source of raw sense data, without order or meaning and, in perception, these data become 'detached (as "stimuli") from the environment and attached (as "sensations") to human subjects' (Ingold 1992: 51). They are then ordered into cultural schemata. The line of argument taken here is akin to parts of that recently advanced by Ingold, which he terms a 'dwelling perspective'. People and environment are constitutive components of the *same* world, which it is unhelpful to think of in terms of a binary nature/culture distinction. In the perception of the world and in the consumption of resources (utilitarian or symbolic) from that world meanings embodied in environmental objects are drawn into the experiences of subjects. Perception of the world and the constitution of that which is important or unimportant to people does not work in terms of a 'blank environmental slate' on which perception and cognition sets to work, but in terms of the historicity of lived experiences in that world. The landscape is an anonymous sculptural form always already fashioned by human agency, never completed, and constantly being added to, and the relationship between people and it is a constant dialectic and process of structuration: the landscape is both medium *for* and outcome *of* action and previous histories of action. Landscapes are experienced in practice, in life activities.

Ingold argues that 'the cultural construction of the environment is not so much a *prelude* to practical action as an (optional) epilogue' and 'culture is a framework not for *perceiving* the world, but for *interpreting* it, to oneself and others' (Ingold 1992: 52–3). It seems unhelpful to polarize, as Ingold appears to do, perception and interpretation, practical activity and the cultural work of explication and discourse. To ask: 'Which comes first: practical activity or cultural knowledge?' is to set up artifical barriers between practical activities and discursive levels of consciousness that go to constitute each other, neither of which is amenable to prioritization. The cultural construction of the environment is both 'prelude' *and* 'epilogue', and it does not necessarily involve 'explication' or 'discourse', as Ingold assumes.

Features of the natural landscape may be held to have provided a symbolic resource of the utmost significance to prehistoric populations. A number of ethnographies of small-scale societies, discussed in Chapter 2, of both hunter–gatherers and subsistence cultivators, indicate that rather than simply providing a backdrop for human action the natural landscape is a cognized form redolent with place names, associations and memories that serve to humanize and enculture landscape, linking together topographical features, trees, rocks, rivers, birds and animals with patterns of human intentionality. Significant locations become crystallized out of the environment through the production and recognition of meanings in particular places and through events that have taken place. Humanized places become fashioned out of the landscape through the recognition of significant qualities in that which has not in itself been culturally produced (rocks, rivers, trees, etc.) by association with current use, past social actions or actions of a mythological character.

It is important not to forget that the contemporary term 'landscape' is highly ideological. Cosgrove and Daniels define landscape as 'a cultural image, a pictorial way of representing, structuring or symbolising surroundings' (Cosgrove and Daniels 1988: 1). Such an image may be structured on canvas, in writing and on the ground through earth, stone and vegetation. Landscapes, in this rather limited definition, are images which are created and read, verbal or non-verbal texts. Raymond Williams (1973: 120) notes that the very idea of landscape implies separation and observation. A concern with landscape is one of patrician control manifested in landscape painting, writing, gardening and architecture. Cosgrove (1984) locates the origins of the idea of landscape in early capitalist Italian Renaissance city states: the city gives birth simultaneously to capitalism and landscape. Landscape is a particular way of seeing, the linear techniques of perspective developed in landscape painting at this time to create a 'realistic' image parallel the development of practices such as cartography, astronomy, land surveying and mapping involving formal geometrical rules. The whole notion of landscape, Cosgrove argues, propagates a visual ideology masking the social forces and relations of production, relations of exploitation and alienation.

Yet in a seemingly contradictory fashion Cosgrove also extols the virtues of landscape as concept and image:

> landscape is a uniquely valuable concept for a humane geography. Unlike *place* it reminds us of our position in the scheme of nature. Unlike *environment* or *space* it reminds us that only through human consciousness and reason is that scheme known to us, and only through technique can we participate as humans in it. At the same time landscape reminds us that geography *is* everywhere, that it is a constant source of beauty and ugliness, of right and wrong and joy and suffering, as much as it is of profit and loss' (Cosgrove 1989: 122).

Daniels (1989), discussing the work of Williams and Berger in relation to landscape and its representation through artworks, brings out a similar tension in their relation to the concept. Representations of landscape have the potential to both obscure and articulate lived experience. In other words landscape as image has both ideological and ontological implications for the way in which we think about the world. Daniels rightly concludes that 'we should beware of attempts to define landscape, to resolve its contradictions; rather we should abide in its duplicity' (Daniels 1989: 218).

It is the ontological connotations of landscape stressed by Cosgrove, in the passage cited above, that make it important to retain the term, to abide in the duplicity of using it at all. As should be clear from the preceding discussions, I reject a notion of landscape as inhering solely in the form of mental representation and cognition. By 'landscape' I want instead to refer to the physical and visual form of the earth as an environment and as a setting in which locales occur and in dialectical relation to which meanings are created, reproduced and transformed. The *appearance* of a landscape is something that is substantial and capable of being described in terms of relief, topography, the flows of contours and rivers, coasts, rocks and soils, and so on. It is most usually clearly defined features, such as mountain peaks, ridges, bogs and plains, that occur in geographical descriptions. The locales in a landscape may be natural features such as bays or inlets on a coastline or high points, or humanly created places such as monuments or settlements. Humanly created locales, I want to argue in this book, draw on *qualities* of landscape to create part of their significance for those who use them, and the perception of the landscape itself may be fundamentally affected by the very situatedness of these locales. A fundamental part of daily experience in non-industrial societies is the physical and biological experience of landscape – earth, water, wood, stone, high places and low places, the wind, rain, sun, stars and sky. The rhythms of the land and the seasons correspond to and are worked into the rhythms of life. A landscape has ontological import because it is lived in and through, mediated, worked on and altered, replete with cultural meaning and symbolism – and not just something looked at or thought about, an object merely for contemplation, depiction, representation and aestheticization.

Powers of Place

Precisely because locales and their landscapes are drawn on in the day-to-day lives and encounters of individuals they possess powers. The spirit of a place may be held to reside in a landscape. Familiarity with the land, being able to read and decode its signs allows individuals to know 'how to go on' at a practical level of consciousness or one that may be discursively formulated. People routinely draw on their stocks of knowledge of the landscape and the locales in which they act to give meaning, assurance and significance to their lives. The place acts dialectically so as to create the people who are of that place. These qualities of locales and landscapes give rise to a feeling of belonging and rootedness and a familiarity, which is not born just out of knowledge, but of *concern* that provides ontological security. They give rise to a power to act and a power to relate that is both liberating and productive.

The relationship of individuals and groups to locales and landscape also has important *perspectival* effects. The experience of these places is unlikely to be equally shared and experienced by all, and the understanding and use of them can be controlled and exploited in systems of domination – a consideration strikingly absent in virtually all phenomenological theory and one that constitutes a major theoretical void. In small-scale societies the major axes of spatial domination are usually organized along the axes of age, gender, kin, and lineage. Knowledge and experience of particular locales and tracts of the landscape may be restricted and hidden from particular individuals and groups. The powers of spatial experience are clearly related to the manner in which they are realized, to whom, when and how. Features of the settings of social interaction may constitute 'disciplinary' spaces through which knowledge is controlled or acquired in a highly structured manner. The ability to control access to and manipulate particular settings for action is a fundamental feature of the operation of power as domination.

Time, Memory and Movement

Human activities become inscribed within a landscape such that every cliff, large tree, stream, swampy area becomes a familiar place. Daily passages through the landscape become biographic encounters for individuals, recalling traces of past activities and previous events and the reading of signs – a split log here, a marker stone there.

All locales and landscapes are therefore embedded in the social and individual times of memory. Their pasts as much as their spaces are crucially constitutive of their presents. Neither space nor time can be understood apart from social practices which serve to bind them together. The human experience of encountering a new place or knowing how to act or go on in a familiar place is intimately bound up with previous experiences. Places are always 'read' or understood in relation to others. While places and movement between them are intimately related to the formation of personal biographies, places themselves may be said to acquire a history, sedimented layers of meaning by virtue of the actions and events that take place in them. Personal biographies, social identities and a biography of place are intimately connected. Memories of previous moves in a landscape are as essential to understanding as they are in playing a game of chess. Remembrance is a process solidified from things and spatial encounters. Movement in the world always involves a loss of place, but the gaining of a fragment of time. It sets up a series of expectations for the paths of the future. Memories continually provide modifications to a sense of place which can never be exactly the same place twice, although there may be ideological attempts to provide 'stability' or perceptual and cognitive fixity to a place, to reproduce sets of dominant meanings, understandings, representations and images.

There is an art of moving in the landscape, a right way (socially constrained) to move around in it and approach places and monuments. Part of the sense of place is the action of approaching it from the 'right' (socially prescribed) direction. To mention just one example here, the Gabbra camel herders of the Kenyan–Ethiopian borderlands undertake ritual pilgrimages and perform periodic rituals at holy mountain sites surrounded by plains. These *jila* journeys are a return to the origin sites of individual Gabbra lineages. The journeys establish spatial linkages between different mountains or mountain peaks and given lineages. Through the journey the lineage becomes 'mapped' in the terrain. The shortest route to a ritual mountain from any point on the plain is not taken but rather a prescribed walk in which it can be approached and seen from the propitious direction (Schlee 1992).

A walk is always a combination of places and times- seasonal and social times. De Certeau (1984: Part III) has described an art of walking which is simultaneously an art of thinking and an art of practice or operating in the world. Movement through space constructs 'spatial stories', forms of narrative understanding. This involves a continuous presencing of previous experiences in present contexts. Spatial knowledge requires the coupling of an accumulated time of memory to overcome an initially hostile and alienating encounter with a new place. Flashes of memory, so to speak, illuminate the occasion.

Pedestrian 'speech acts' may be likened to the speech acts of language. Walking is a process of appropriation of the topographical system, as speaking is an appropriation of language. It is a spatial acting out of place, as the speech act is an acoustic acting out of language. Walking, like language use, implies relationality in terms of an overall system of differences. It is a movement with reference to a differentiated series of locales, just as language is constituted as a system of differences between signs – 'dog' is dog because it is not cat, and so on (de Certeau 1984: 98).

A spatial order of walking can be characterized in terms of an order of possibilities – various ways in which an actor can move, and a series of restrictions, for example walls or other boundaries inhibiting passage. A walker actualizes only some of the possibilities, which may be relatively open or closed in terms of the overall 'grammatical' system. These possibilities remain only as potentialities in so far as they only exist in the act of their realization through movement in the world. Through movement parts of the system – places or paths – are ignored, condemned to inertia, while others are activated through use or presence. De Certeau goes further than this to refer to a 'rhetoric' and 'tropes' of walking, which can be likened to turns of phrase. An art of 'turning phrases' provides an analogy for an individual's following or diverging from paths, both of them constituting ways of being, thinking and operating in the world. Synecdoche is an art of speaking in which a part stands for a whole (sail for ship, tree for forest, monument for landscape). In walking a street may substitute for a community, a path for a network of paths. The part is expanded into something more, a totality. Asyndeton, an art of speaking involving the suppression of linking words such as conjunctions between or within sentences, finds a spatial expression in the cutting out of places. Synecdoche then creates spatial densities; asyndeton undermines or cuts through continuities.

> A space treated in this way and shaped by practices is transformed into enlarged singularities and separate islands. Through these swellings, shrinkages, and fragmentations, that is through these rhetorical operations a spatial phrasing of an analogical (composed of juxtaposed citations) and elliptical (made of gaps, lapses and allusions) type is created. For the technological system of a coherent and totalizing space that is 'linked' and simultaneous, the figures of pedestrian rhetoric substitute trajectories ... [which are a] stylistic metamorphosis of space (de Certeau 1984: 101–2).

The important aspect of this argument is its revelation of an art of walking as simultaneously an art of consciousness, habit and practice, that is both constrained by place and landscape and constitutive of them. Walking is the medium and outcome of a spatial practice, a mode of existence in the world. The analogy can be taken further in the consideration of paths.

Paths, Inscriptions, Temporality

If writing solidifies or objectifies speech into a material medium, a text, which can be read and interpreted, an analogy can be drawn between a pedestrian speech act and its inscription or writing on the ground in the form of the path or track. Both are sedimented traces of activity, and both provide ways to be followed. A strong path is inscribed through a forest or across a tract of heathland through a multitude of pedestrian speech acts that keep it open; a strong text is also one that is kept open, read many times. Just as the writing of a text is dependent on previous texts (it has the characteristic of intertextuality), the creation or maintenance of a path is dependent on a previous networking of movements in particular, and reiterated directions through a landscape; it works in relation to a previous set of precedents.

The metaphor of the path is a common one in many small-scale societies, and refers beyond itself to patterns of activity and social organization. A path may be a way of doing something as method, technique, pattern or strategy. In Oceania and Indonesia fishing techniques, oratorical skills, patterns of exchange and strategies of warfare are also termed 'paths'. Paths are also fundamentally to do with establishing and maintaining social linkages and relations between individuals, groups and political units. Social paths and the paths followed through the forest may become overgrown through lack of use in any particular (physical or social) direction.

Parmentier (1987: 109–11) notes three general features of the semantic fields of paths on the island of Belau derived from reflections on movements made along them. First, points linked by a clear path have achieved a degree of structural homology and hence positive cultural identity. The points linked by paths share sets of common elements – sacred stones, trees, artefact depositions, names and titles referred to in myths and stories and linked to the activities of ancestors who stopped on the journey which created the path. Second, linked places on paths can be understood in terms of sequential precedence, a hierarchy of ancestral origin points from which paths radiate to others. Priority in time is linked to the ceremonial precedence and power of places linked by paths. Third, paths structure experiences of the places they link, they help to establish a sense of linear order. A path brings forth possibilities for repeated actions within prescribed confines. Only a high-ranking or wealthy person is likely to be daring enough to invent a path or plant a relationship not established before. Such action is most usually the domain of the gods or heroic ancestors. Expert knowledge of ancient paths is part of the responsibility of chiefs who can harness great power by narrating stories recounting previous patterns of ancestral movements (ibid.: 114–15).

A journey along a path can be claimed to be a paradigmatic cultural act, since it is following in the steps inscribed by others whose steps have worn a conduit for movement which becomes the correct or 'best way to go'. Spatiotemporal linkages thus established become obvious templates for future movements and the maintenance of relationships. Linked places along the journey may be read in terms of temporal relationships of precedence and power. There is usually a good reason for following in a particular direction linking places in a serial trajectory, and the more people who have shared in the purpose of the path the more important it becomes. Paths form an essential medium for the routing of social relations, connecting up spatial impressions with temporally inscribed memories.

Spatial Stories, Landscape and the Arts of Narrative

In movement on a path through the landscape something is constantly slipping away and something is constantly gained in a relational tactile world of impressions, signs, sights, smells and physical sensations. To understand a landscape truly it must be felt, but to convey some of this feeling to others it has to be talked about, recounted, or written and depicted. In the process of movement a landscape unfolds or unravels before an observer. Beyond one chain of hills another is revealed; the view from a locale makes sense of its positioning. The importance and significance of a place can only be appreciated as part of movement from and to it in relation to others, and the act of moving may be as important as that of arriving. The path may be a symbol not only of interconnectedness and social relations but of movement through life. If places are read and experienced in relation to others and through serial movement along the axes of paths it follows that an art of understanding of place, movement and landscape must fundamentally be a narrative understanding involving a presencing of previous experiences in present contexts. Spatial and textual stories are embedded in one another.

Narrative structure and emplotment can easily be claimed to have ontological significance for human existence, to be as universal as language itself. It is precisely because narrative is seemingly so 'natural' a part of human existence that it is both an important resource for analysis and understanding and something whose non-critical use as *merely* description is something to be wary of. A critical understanding of spatial narrative requires that we investigate precisely why we prefer some plots or configurations of things rather than others. In other words attention must be played to the manner in which the story is creatively orchestrated, how it guides, and what it passes through.

Narrative is a means of understanding and describing the world in relation to agency. It is a means of linking locales, landscapes, actions, events and experiences together providing a synthesis of heterogeneous phenomena. In its simplest form it involves a story and a story-teller. In its mimetic or phenomenological form narrative seeks to capture action not just through description but as a form of re-description. Events are given meaning through their configuration into a whole requiring the emplotment of action. A narrative must of necessity always be written from a certain point of view. In relation to the past and written from the standpoint of the present, narrative structures play a similar role to metaphor – they describe the world in fresh ways, bringing new meanings and new senses, and the productivity is, in principle, endless. Ricoeur (1983) rightly emphasizes the poetic qualities of narratives in producing configurations of events and objects that go far beyond a simple matter of succession, i.e. this occurs after or because of that.

De Certeau (1984) points out that every story not only involves some kind of temporal movement, but is also a spatial practice. Stories organize walks, making a journey as the feet perform it, organizing places by means of the displacements that are described. They are part of a human labour that transforms an abstract homogeneous space into place – 'you go round the corner, turn left and you'll see...'. In other words the story is a discursive articulation of a spatializing practice, a bodily itinerary and routine. Spatial stories are about the operations and practices which constitute places and locales. The map, by contrast, involves a stripping away of these things: 'it alone remains on the stage. The tour describers have disappeared' (de Certeau 1984:

121). If stories are linked with regularly repeated spatial practices they become mutually supportive, and when a story becomes sedimented into the landscape, the story and the place dialectically help to construct and reproduce each other. Places help to recall stories that are associated with them, and places only exist (as named locales) by virtue of their emplotment in a narrative. Places, like persons, have biographies inasmuch as they are formed, used and transformed in relation to practice. It can be argued that stories acquire part of their mythic value and historical relevance if they are rooted in the concrete details of locales in the landscape, acquiring material reference points that can be visited, seen and touched.

If naming is an act of construction of landscape, constituting an origin point for it, then narratives introduce temporality, making locales markers of individual and group experiences. Basso (1984), in an excellent paper, demonstrates how individual Apaches experience oral narratives: 'the land is always stalking people. The land makes people live right' (Annie Peaches, cited in Basso 1984: 21). Narratives establish bonds between people and features of the landscape such as mountains, creating moral guidance for activity. Both land and language are equally symbolic resources drawn on to foster correct social behaviour and values. In narratives geographical features of the landscape act as mnemonic pegs on which moral teachings hang. The landscape is full of named locations that act so as to fuse time and space. Through the use of historical tales events are located at named points, and the tales themselves are about correct codes of moral conduct. 'Shooting someone with a story' is relating a historical tale about misconduct that reflects back on their misdemeanours, a tale that becomes anchored in space through specifying a named geographical location where the event took place. Stories are intimately connected with physical places on the land, fused with geological elements: 'you cannot *live* in that land without asking or looking at or noticing a boulder or rock. And there's always a story' (Silko 1981: 69, cited in Basso 1984). Features of the landscape become deeply symbolic of cultural lifeworlds, omnipresent moral forces rather than mere physical presences (Basso 1984: 46). Through narratives conceptions of the land affect the way in which the Apache think of themselves and vice versa.

Conclusion

A landscape is a series of named locales, a set of relational places linked by paths, movements and narratives. It is a 'natural' topography perspectivally linked to the existential Being of the body in societal space. It is a cultural code for living, an anonymous 'text' to be read and interpreted, a writing pad for inscription, a scape of and for human praxis, a mode of dwelling and a mode of experiencing. It is invested with powers, capable of being organized and choreographed in relation to sectional interests, and is always sedimented with human significances. It is story and telling, temporality and remembrance. Landscape is a signifying system through which the social is reproduced and transformed, explored and structured – process organized. Landscape, above all, represents a means of conceptual ordering that stresses relations. The concept emphasizes a conventional means of doing so, the stress is on similarity to control the undermining nature of difference, of multivocal code, found in the concepts of place or locale. A concept of place privileges difference and singularity; a concept of landscape is more holistic, acting so as to encompass rather than exclude. It is to a discussion of various ways in which landscapes may be organized that the next chapter turns.

Chapter 2

The Social Construction of Landscape in Small-Scale Societies: Structures of Meaning, Structures of Power

Introduction

In this chapter I want to discuss relationships established between people and the landscape in small-scale 'traditional' societies, reviewing some of the discussions in the ethnographic literature relating to hunter–fisher–gatherers and subsistence cultivators. The aim is to underline the affective, emotional and symbolic significance of the landscape and highlight some of the similarities and differences in the relationship between people and the land, and the manner in which it is culturally constructed, invested with powers and significances, and appropriated in widely varying 'natural' environments and social settings.

A caveat is in order: in general terms the anthropological literature, in contrast with that of human geography, is not exactly replete with discussions of the significance of landscape. It is rare to even find an entry in an index referring to 'landscape', or use of the term in a book, article or chapter title. Landscape has remained a neglected area of study, and detailed accounts are few and far between. Two books, currently in press as I write, are exceptions which prove the rule (Bender 1993; Hirsch and O'Hanlon, in press). One, I think erroneous, conclusion that might be drawn from this is that the landscape simply does not matter, or the category is irrelevant to understanding the manner in which populations in small-scale societies interact with, understand and relate to their physical surroundings.

However, a great number of texts do make mention of the significance of the land. For example, Barth in his introduction to a monograph on the Baktaman of Papua New Guinea notes that 'Baktaman are highly oriented towards *space* in ordering their experience. The vocabulary and grammar of their language impel a speaker constantly to specify relative location (distance, direction, and above/below on a slope) of observer and actor in describing events; and they have a variety of means to describe landscape features and shapes. There is also a wealth of place names of differing order by which to designate area and specific location. Places also serve to recall events in the past – stories and anecdotes that I was unable to elicit in conversation in the men's house would suddenly surface in the forest with the opening 'this is the spot where ...' (Barth 1975: 18). Yet despite the evident significance of the land for the Baktaman this remains unelaborated in Barth's otherwise excellent account. Similarly, although Hugh-Jones (1979) devotes a great deal of attention to discussing the paramount symbolic, cosmological and social significance of the river for the Pirá-paraná of North-west Amazonia, it remains uncontextualized in terms of a wider concept of the landscape, its topographic and physiographic features, cultural and symbolic significances through and by means of which these peoples live out their lives.

Turnbull (1961, 1965, 1983), discussing the Mbuti hunter–fisher–gatherers of the Ituri rain forest, Zaïre, emphasizes the generalized significance of the forest as provider, spiritual entity and mystical force. He contrasts the Mbuti attitude to the forest with that of the Bantu farmers, who fear and loathe it, people it with evil forces and constantly struggle to maintain their hard-won clearings against its encroachment. To the Mbuti the forest is a vital life-engendering and empowering force, to the Bantu a symbol of everything they are struggling against. For the Mbuti the land is a subject of labour, for the Bantu an object of labour. The Mbuti are constantly moving about and changing their encampments within the space of the forest. They view their world from the perspective of following and creating tracks and paths through the forest. The Bantu, on the other hand, have a fixed relationship to their environment, viewed from the vantage point of the village clearing. The ordered life of the village is surrounded by the chaotic, malevolent and unseen world of the forest into which they are loath to venture. Yet this is about as far as Turnbull's fascinating account goes on the subject of the landscape, and it would be unwise to generalize from it, viz: all hunter–gatherers tend to view the land from a decentred perspective in which many places within it are of equal relevance, while farmers have a more centred or concentric frame of reference, focused on the village looking out. These are more likely to represent two extremes along a continuum of variation of cultural responses.

While the significance of the landscape, glossed by the use of terms such as 'space' or 'environment' in the anthropological literature, receives widespread acknowledgement as constituting a fundamental part of existential existence among both hunters and farmers, it is rarely foregrounded in any discussion (with some exceptions, see below). Why this apparent lacuna? As indicated in Chapter 1, the answer would seem to be that 'landscape' is an unstable category, sitting uneasily between opposed ecological or 'naturalistic' and ideological or 'culturological' approaches to human society in the literature. In my view this is precisely the contemporary interest and power of employing such a category today. It may provocatively be used to draw together approaches that tend to be held apart in the literature or are conceptualized as occupying radically different domains of human action and experience which are only tangentially related. Rather than attempting any extensive discussion of the literature as a whole in so far as it explicitly or otherwise addresses the issue of landscape, its physical forms, perception and meanings, an enormous and possibly not very illuminating task, I have decided to concentrate in this chapter on a number of specific examples drawn from widely separated geographical locations.

It would be difficult to find two more contrasting areas in terms of topography, climate and resource availability than Australia and Alaska and subarctic North America; but despite these differences the existential relationship between the Koyukon, the Mistassini Cree and the Aborigines and the landscape is remarkably similar in some respects, a point whose significance I attempt to emphasize in the discussion below of the relationship between hunter–fisher–gatherer communities and the land. In discussing subsistence cultivators my examples are drawn from the Tewa of New Mexico and a number of Melanesian societies.

Hunter–Fisher–Gatherers and Landscape

Landscapes of the Dreamtime
It is impossible to consider the Australian Aborigines adequately without considering landscape, so strong is their relationship

with it. As Morphy points out (1993: 206) this appears to be one of those cases in which indigenous perceptions, as opposed to theoretical preoccupations, have actively and consistently *determined* rather than *constrained* the nature of anthropological representations of society. The Aboriginal landscape is one replete with a highly elaborate totemic geography linking together place and people. Formed in the Dreamtime, the landscape provides an ancestral map for human activity. It is sedimented in history and sentiment. The landscape is not something 'natural' and opposed to people, but totally socialized. It is a symbolic form, a series of signs relating to the ancestral past on which people draw in day-to-day experience and through which they live. According to Stanner (1965: 215), the grounding basis of Aboriginal mythology and enduring proof of its correctness was the evidence of *design* in the world in the sense of pattern, shape, form and structure, which was itself proof of *intent*. This design was manifest in the landscape itself, its topographic features and physiographic patterns, flora and fauna, constituting a vast sign system whose significance was to be read and interpreted. In the process populations emotionally bound themselves to the land and the design inherent in its ordering.

Each group of Aborigines originally moved around a particular area of territory in a traditional pattern, exploiting the fauna and flora of their environments. A striking feature of Aboriginal life that cannot be over-emphasized is the intense personal bond between groups and their home territories. Attachment to and knowledge of a particular stretch of land was a fundamental part of existence. The desert, described by Strehlow (1965), Berndt (1972) and others, is by no means uniformly arid, and includes low undulating ridges, sand-dunes covered by grass and scrub, claypans and shallow creek beds, stretches of dry sand-hills, expanses of pebbles and rocky outcrops. During wet seasons the whole area abounds in edible plants, roots and game. In protracted dry seasons populations are forced to aggregate close to permanent water sources. A great deal of traditional Aboriginal life was focused on the theme of water. Berndt notes that the Balgo population of the southern Kimberleys of Western Australia distinguish eight physiographic features which are water-producing, including soaks, temporary and virtually permanent creeks, swamps and rockholes (Berndt 1972: 179). People identify specific tracts of land as their 'country' not just in terms of an area with demarcated boundaries, but much more intimately in terms of specific locales, such as waterholes, sand ridges, claypans and camping grounds. Specific sites are claimed to belong to individual social units, and the total of these constitutes the territory of a group. Territories are made up of significant sites, rather than being conceived in a more abstract spatialized manner as relatively well-defined areas of land with boundaries *containing* sites. As Ingold puts it: 'land does not contain sites; rather the sites contain the land' (Ingold 1986: 150). People do not, therefore, restrict themselves to delimited territorial areas, but may wander over areas claimed in the same way by other groups. Most usually groups do not range beyond 300 km. from their traditional territorial area.

According to Dixon (1976) tribal boundaries in Australia are of two basic kinds. Over large tracts of Australia they are centred on waterlines, separated by tracts of drier relatively infertile country along which imprecisely defined boundaries occur. In less arid country they may more typically lie along river courses themselves. In a discussion of Yolngu social boundaries Williams (1982) comments that they are always marked by natural features, many of which may be far from obvious to an outsider. The more obvious boundaries are related to prominent land forms such as hills, mountains, cliffs, streams, rivers and watersheds. Other boundaries may be marked by changes in gradient on a slope or changes in vegetation or soil or rock types (Williams 1982: 141–3). Combinations embracing different types of physical characteristics may be employed. A boundary may be located, for example, just below the crest of a hill, where a slight change in gradient occurs in association with a change in soil type or vegetation. In general terms a bounded area of land bears the name of a dominant and striking physiographic feature which is the primary referent point, and may be the most important site, such as a large pool of water in a billabong (intermittent stream). Boundaries of coastal land defined by physical features such as clusters of rocks jutting out into the sea or even changes in the colours of offshore waters are used to extend land boundaries outward across the sea to the horizon (ibid.: 144–5).

Boundaries, as with virtually everything else in the Aboriginal system of knowledge, are related to mythologies. Strehlow (1965) shows how the boundaries of each *njinana* (local section group) of the Aranda in the Western desert were demarcated by episodes in myths which relate the points at which ancestors travelling across the landscape reached boundary points. Boundary points were known as 'barriers', and beyond them myths could not be told, songs sung nor a series of ceremonies be performed by members of a section area who shared these traditions with neighbours (Strehlow 1965: 138).

The whole landscape is criss-crossed by a multitude of tracks following the main watercourses and extending in a variety of directions from one site to the next, incorporating all topographical features that are symbolically and economically significant. Mythical beings created these tracks, and present-day populations move along them while hunting and gathering. Topographic features of the landscape act not only as boundary-marking devices of varying types and orientation points on tracks, but play a central role as a sign system and are crucial in the formation of Aboriginal concepts of creation, spiritual power and world order (Berndt 1972, 1974, 1976; Morphy 1991, Morphy n.d.; Munn 1970, 1986; Stanner 1966). The landscape both constitutes a referent for much of the symbolism and acts as a sign system for mythological events. It simultaneously passes on and encodes information about the ancestral past and is integral to the message. The landscape is the fundamental reference system in which individual consciousness of the world and social identities are anchored. Emotional ties with the land are obviously related to economic dependencies, the exigencies of gathering and hunting; but just as significantly to mythic beings, who create and sustain the fertility of the land and stimulate the natural increase of species. For the Aborigines the earth came into being as a result of the actions of the ancestors. These ancestors continue to exist in spirit form, and in the era of creation they travelled the earth, and in their doings created the topographical features. The movements of the ancestral snake created the meanderings of the watercourses, the blood of the ancestors formed red ochre and so on. Objects used by the ancestors, such as baskets or digging sticks, may be left behind when they went into the earth. Ancestors may therefore leave behind a wide variety of indications of their presence, and are not uniquely related to any one type of transformation or metamorphosis. The landscape was one in which the ancestors hunted and gathered, and so every aspect of it has generalized ancestral connotations. It contains the bodies of the ancestors inside it and is also the metamorphosed forms of

the ancestors, the tracks they made and the imprint of their bodies. For example, where an ancestor sat down a waterhole may be
created. The ancestors both created the world and interacted with
it. They gave birth to human beings and their correct form of
social organization and religious practices. Ancestors may be
wholly human or part human and part non-human, male or
female. Their number is indefinite. The initial naming of ancestral
sites is attributed to the ancestors, like their physical creation, and
the names of the sites may be thought of as ancestors' proper
names. 'Ancestral naming and transformation create a determinate fixed phenomenal reality grounded in the specificity of form
and verbal sign (proper names)' (Munn 1970: 143).

The tracks of the ancestors cross the territories where the
Aborigines live, and each patrilodge controls a number of tracks
and the ancestors associated with them. Clans can be distinguished on the basis of the particular nexus of dreaming tracks
they control. Munn notes that 'narratives bind events to an objective geographical space through the listing of named places. This
spatial localization yields the basic symbolism of transgenera-
tional continuity, since the sense of continuity over the generations is "carried" in the experience of the country as a network of
objectively identifiable places, the prime "givens" of the external
environment' (Munn 1986: 214–15). The landscape is thus filled
with meaning and memories, redolent with the actions of the
past. The ancestral beings fixed in the land itself, in the trees,
hills, lakes, sand-dunes and watercourses, become timeless referent points for the living, according to Morphy (n.d.), outside the
politics of daily life. Through day-to-day life activities individuals learn of this ordered world of ancestral activity, which
becomes part and parcel of their experience of place.

Berndt has described in detail the complexity of the dreaming
tracks or 'water-lines' and their relationship to the topography.
Three major tracks in a small slice of Balgo territory in the
Western desert contained no less than 73 different named locations (Fig. 2.1). These locales are 'big names', each of which may
be associated with a number of 'smaller names' that are no less
significant (Fig. 2.2). At any place part of the essence of the
mythic being referred to is materially manifested in one way or
another. On Elcho island in north-eastern Arnhem land Berndt
records 164 named places with ancestral associations, noting that
this is only a partial list. Here, where the main economic resource

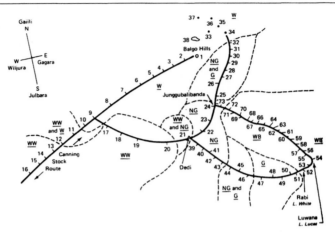

Figure 2.1. Dreamtime tracks, Balgo territory, Western Australia. Three major tracks are shown. Numbered topographic locales are all 'big name' places with a variety of mythological and ancestral associations, e.g. 6: Gilanggilang lake where the great Rainbow serpent emerged; 21: Dedi rockhole associated with Wilbin, wild cat.

Source: Berndt 1972, Fig. 5.2.
By kind permission of Holt, Rinehart and Winston.

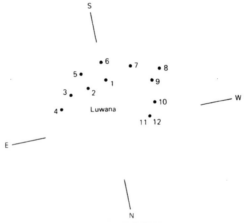

Figure 2.2. 'Small names' within the big name locality Luwana Spring or Lake Lucas (Fig. 2.1 No. 54). Each of these 12 names relates to a specific topographic feature, e.g. site 1 is a soak and rockhole associated with Wadi Bududjuru, a small kangaroo rat who sits within a hole at this place and is represented by a stone into which he turned.

Source: Berndt 1972: Fig. 5.3.
By kind permission of Holt, Rinehart and Winston.

was fish, the concentration of named locales is coastal, with relatively few inland sites (Berndt 1976: 147–55). Local people belong
to a territory and to sites within it by means of patrilineal descent,
and use the word *djaga* in relation to it, meaning 'looking after' or
'cherishing', the same word used by parents in relation to their
children (Berndt 1976: 156). Thus all persons are linked in an
enduring way with a series of locales, and can never of their own
accord sever this association. Temporarily unoccupied tracts of
territory will always have *someone* 'looking after' the named sites
(Berndt 1972: 193; 1976: 160). This is not a matter of ownership,
but rather that living populations act as custodians. The sites are
visible and tangible expressions of segments of myth told in stories and in song. These myths not only concern the activities of
the ancestors, but also encode information about locales vital to
group survival locating in space sources of water and other characteristics of the environment relevant to its economic exploitation. Myths 'represent *in toto* the experience and heritage of the
people concerned, a basis for social as well as economic living'
(Berndt 1972: 188).

   Perhaps the most striking example of topography embodying
living mythology is Ayers Rock in the middle of Australia, an
enormous dome-shaped rock monolith with a flattened top rising
almost vertically from an extensive desert plain (Fig. 2.3). Ten different totemic mythical beings created the topography of the
rock. Most of the southern face was created by a battle between
liru (poisonous snakes) and *kunia* (carpet snakes). Minor portions
were also created by *linga* (sand lizards) and *metalungana* (sleepy-
lizards). The activities of the *mala* (hare-wallabies) created most
of the northern face, with other ancestors creating highly specific
parts of the topography. Other ancestors created the western face,
such as the marsupial mole, who was responsible for creating pot
holes and caves (Mountford 1965) (Fig. 2.4). The mythic associations of the rock are of two basic types. The first relate to ancestors who rested and performed activities there and then passed
on for hundreds of kilometres along their dreaming tracks. The
second refer to ancestors who originated at the rock and stayed
there. There is virtually no place on the surface of the rock,
whether it be a striated surface, boulder, declivity, rockhole or
cave that is not a named ancestral locality (Fig. 2.5). Ayers rock
was not only a total mythological fact for the surrounding populations, a perceptual field encoding knowledge of the world, but

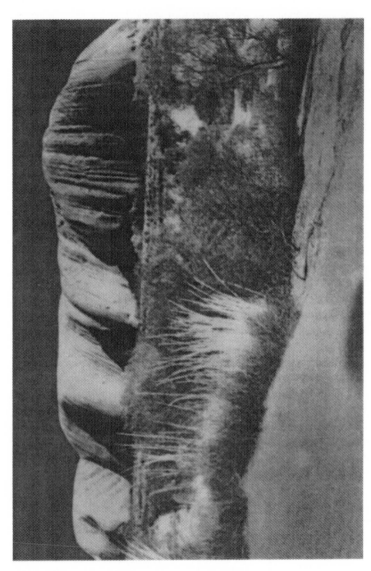

Figure 2.3. Ayers rock from the south.   Source: Mountford 1965: Plate 3B. By kind permission of East-West Center Press.

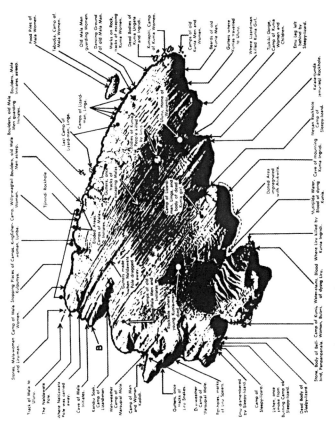

Figure 2.4. The totemic geography of Ayers rock.

Source: Mountford 1965: Fig. 3. By kind permission of East-West Center Press.

Figure 2.5. Tracks of fleeing carpet snakes, Ayers rock.
Source: Mountford 1965: Plate 28A. By kind permission of East-West Center Press.

a focus for linking present populations to the past ancestral forces, involving rock engraving, painting and initiation rites. Both the external surfaces of the rock were decorated at specific points with ancestral associations, and twelve caves on the northern and southern sides contain paintings depicting dreamtime events (Mountford 1965: 157 ff.).

Morphy (1991, n.d.) describes the Yolngu of North-east Arnhem Land as having a particularly rich vocabulary for topographic and environmental description which serves to segregate environmental zones which are linked both to seasonal resource exploitation and the mythological system. There is a close correspondence between topographical zone and ancestral track, and the distribution of ancestral beings is related to that of natural species. Major ritual sites correspond closely to paths of movement. The dreamtime tracks, as elsewhere, tend to follow the watercourses, and the greatest density of mythological activities is generally associated with major camp sites. The landscape is thus represented in myth and represents the myth. It is a mnemonic for past generations and a means of establishing continuity with the past. Time becomes collapsed into space, in that the time it took ancestral beings to take their journeys is never a part of the myth. Time becomes a sequence of named places without the 'befores' and 'afters'. Disrepectful behaviour towards the land and its species can cause illness or death.

Layton (n.d.) discusses the intense personal and biographical relationship between people, the land and ancestral beings in central Australia. While places are intimately related to ancestral activity, so are the living. All individuals are first identified with one of the *Tjukurpa* beings at birth according to where the *puli* (stub of their umbilical cord) fell off, and their personalities are expected to follow those of the ancestors of which they are an embodied part. In this manner people are identified with places, a connection which cannot be severed. Persons 'hold' land by means of this intimate personal association and by continuing to live in and care for it. Proof of this 'holding of the land' is bound up with detailed knowledge of and interpretation of physiographic features linked to ancestral activities. Failure to protect songs, ceremonies and sacred objects is equivalent to giving the land away. In other words the ancestral past has to be continually brought into and related to activity in the present. Anyone who regularly forages in a region needs to be intimately acquainted with ancestral lore, ceremony, song and sacred objects, which become the grounding basis for all life movements. People cannot 'hold' a country as children, but only when they have become 'big'. Those who own an estate have pre-eminent rights to it by (i) controlling access to it through controlling knowledge of ancestral lore associated with the terrain; (ii) demanding something from people from another country who temporarily come to hunt there; (iii) punishing trespassers on sacred sites (Layton n.d.). At death the living must relinquish their claims to a country, and their descendants must take care of it, perform the correct ceremonies and guard the ancestral relics. Alienation of any part of the country from its rightful owners and their heirs is a violation of the entire moral order, a desecration (Munn 1970: 150).

Physiographic features of the landscape play a crucial role in ritual practices. Within any clan territory localized sacred sites occur to which unauthorized access is forbidden. Only those who know the land can call and prepare ceremonies. Sacred sites always occur near to water, and while access to the water itself is not physically defended the sites are. Senior men only may visit these sites, take care of them, and perform rituals. Rock art locales form one such category of sites. Layton (n.d.) notes that depictions of the landscape in Australian Aboriginal art are notable for the bird's-eye view they adopt, a decentred perspective in which numerous points have equal value. Sacred sites and ancestral tracks linking them become laid out as on a map, but these 'maps' have much more in common with the sensuous places of medieval 'cartography' than they do with a Euclidean geometric space of modern cartographic representation.

Painting rocks was an important part of a process by which populations could tap into ancestral powers at specific topographical locations. Sites of particular importance in representations of landscape frequently refer to the places where the ancestors came out of and (having grown tired) went back into the land, between these two events creating their dreaming tracks and localized features of the topography. Munn (1973, 1986) regards the processes of 'coming out' and 'going into' the land (an inside/outside distinction) as a fundamental principle of Walbiri cosmology that is used to explain and structure the spatiotemporal ordering of human existence. Each of the Aranda section areas contained at least one important ceremonial centre at which ancestors are believed to have emerged from the ground to

populate the surrounding countryside. All the main mythological characters associated with emergence from these sacred sites
were revealed through dramatic performances re-enacting ancestral doings, and each site had its own ceremonial cycle involving
the revelation of sacred objects, songs, rites, poetry, dance and
drama (Strehlow 1965: 140). The ancestral beings had the power
of bringing into existence the plants and animals of their totem
when induced to 'emerge' by the rites. Having created the land
their continuous presence ensured its regeneration.

In the art of the Walbiri the circle is the locus out of which the
Dreaming emerges and finally returns. The circle and the line
provide a kind of spatial and conceptual model linking the
dreamtime with the present. The circle (with female sexual connotations) is the present-day country, with the dreamtime ancestors at the centre and hidden inside it. The line conjoined to it
(with male sexual connotations) is the path or track moving
beyond the boundaries of place into the landscape beyond, representing a constant association between past and present (Fig. 2.6).
In more general terms an inside/outside distinction is crucial in
understanding Walbiri concepts of and relationships to land. The

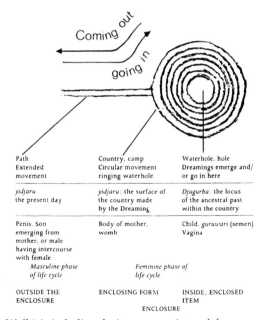

Path	Country, camp	Waterhole, hole
Extended	Circular movement	Dreamings emerge and/
movement	ringing waterhole	or go in here
yidjaru	*yidjaru*: the surface of	*Djugurba*: the locus
the present day	the country made	of the ancestral past
	by the Dreaming	within the country
Penis. Son	Body of mother,	Child, *guruwari* (semen)
emerging from	womb	Vagina
mother, or male		
having intercourse		
with female		
Masculine phase	*Feminine phase of*	
of life cycle	*life cycle*	
OUTSIDE THE	ENCLOSING FORM	INSIDE: ENCLOSED
ENCLOSURE		ITEM
	ENCLOSURE	

Figure 2.6. Walbiri circle-line design as cosmic model.
Source: Munn 1973: Fig. 8. By kind permission of Oxford University Press

	A	B	C
South	4	4	4
	3	7	5
North	2	8	6
	1		1

Feature Block

A   Beach, Female, Nyapililngu, Sandhills, *Burrkun*.
B   Lake, *Marrawili*.
C   Bush, Male, *Guwak*, Sandbank, *Burrkun*.

Meanings Associated with Loci in the Manggalili Template.

1.   North end of lake, gullies in the sandhills, *burrkun*.
2.   Nyapililngu, *burrkun* complex.
3.   Nyapililngu, *burrkun* complex.
4.   *Marrawili* tree, cloud, *guwak*.
5.   Wild plum tree grove, *burrkun* complex.
6.   Cashew tree grove, ngaarra ceremony ground, *burrkun*.
7.   Lake, emu, spears, menstrual blood.
8.   Dry lake bed, emus and spears.

Figure 2.7. Landscape and meanings in Yolngu art. Nyapililngu on the sand dunes. Artist: Bokarra. Clan: Manggalili.

Source: Morphy 1991: Fig. 10.9.
By kind permission of the author and University of Chicago Press.

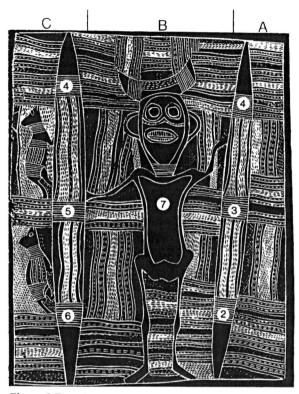

Figure 2.7. *cont.*

dreamtime ancestors still exist inside the earth or under the ground, they are 'covered over' and lie beneath the visible physical surfaces of the land. Art applied to the body or to the surfaces of rocks may, in the context of ceremonies, act so as to 'pull out' ancestral forces (Munn 1973: 198). In increase rites ancestral forces have generative powers which serve to replenish the land. For these rites to be fully effective they had to take place at the original geographical sites (Strehlow 1970: 132).

This inside/outside distinction is a prominent theme in some Aboriginal body art and in barkcloth paintings. Yolngu paintings refer simultaneously to mythological events and topographic features. They both record in visual form a narrative of dreamtime events and present a 'map' of a particular area of land. The landscape created by ancestral actions provides the primary medium for encoding mythological events by ordering them in space, and boundaries and design elements in the paintings refer to this landscape (Fig. 2.7); but, as Morphy points out, the ordering of landscape representations in art and in mental representations and understandings of it is a product of continual interpretations and reinterpretations of place. The positions of places 'correspond to the relative positions of places in the landscape ... but the topographical plotting of positions would produce a very different shape' (Morphy 1991: 237). Landscape and art are both models *of* and models *for* reality, i.e. they are both ordered by something beyond themselves (the landscape as it actually exists) and serve to order that external reality and make sense of it.

One particular type of art, X-ray paintings, depict the internal body organs and bones of ancestral beings at an 'outside' denotative level of meaning. At another 'inside' level of meaning they refer to spatial relationships between important topographic features of clan lands. As Taylor puts it 'the metaphors of these paintings express the way Kunwinjku (Aborigines of western Arnhem Land) conceive of the spatial organization of sites in their lands in terms of an abstract model of the divided yet organically related body parts of the ancestral being that created those lands' (Taylor 1989: 381). There is an intimate connection between body parts of the ancestral being in these paintings and locales of significance in the landscape. This mode of experiencing the world may even extend to the human body itself, through painting designs on it and even in relation to features such as birthmarks' being seen as equivalent to sacred sites within clan lands. The body becomes a metaphor for the topographic organization of clan lands. The significance of landscape is thus inscribed not only in day-to-day encounters with its topographic and physiographic features but in portable and non-portable art and in relation to the scars, marks, painting and surfaces of individual human bodies. It would indeed be hard to find a more encompassing sensibility of the relationship between biography, identity and place than this. Since every person carries within him- or herself a life force ultimately derived from ancestral powers, living populations and ancestral forces are inseparably connected. People do not, for example, actively create designs in artworks; but these designs are passed to them through dreams and are derived from the ancestors. Among the Walbiri, women who sleep together may share the same *yawalyu* designs (Munn 1986).

Taçon (1991) has discussed the manner in which the land and its ancestral significances may be actively appropriated through technologies such as systems of stone-tool production and use. The most significant tools, such as stone axes and spear points, controlled and used by men, embodied ancestral powers. A large number of these ancestors turned into stone at their final resting point. The Rainbow Serpent, one of the most potent of the ancestors in western Arnhem Land, swallowed other ancestors and then was forced to vomit their bones, forming rocky sandstone and quartzite escarpments. Quarrying stone for axes is, therefore, quarrying the bones of the ancestors. The axes are themselves formed from ancestral bones – hence their potency. Quartz tools are particularly potent, as brightness and iridescence are highly valued. Objects and substances that shimmer and 'emit' light, such as quartz, white pigment, fat and blood, are spiritually charged with power (Morphy 1989; Taçon 1991). It is not surprising that quarries were dangerous places, and access to them and their products was tightly controlled in many cases. The killing power of a stone tool is significantly linked to its ancestral source, and it is the power within it that saps the life out of the victim, causing a searing, burning pain (Jones 1990: 27, cited in Taçon 1991: 203–4). Stone is considered to be a male substance, while the earth and its products, such as pigments used for painting, are gendered as female. Ceremonial objects could be empowered by painting, which created a symbolic linkage between male and female essences. By contrast, tools used for killing would be dulled through decoration. It was 'necessary that their "male" qualities not be covered over so that they remain potent to penetrate flesh and, in the process, to be "painted" with blood' (Taçon 1991: 205). Stone and bone were both symbols of persistence, and hence it is not surprising that clefts and holes in rock escarpments were frequently used for secondary burial, a placing of the bones of the dead back inside the bones of the ancestors.

The landscape constitutes for the Aborigines a fundamental form of mediation, in which the experience of self is rooted in the objectified forms of ancestral transformations. Human subjectivity is constituted in relation to the land. There is a constant linkage effected between subject and object, object and subject, which provides a sense of an enduring moral and social order. The land is both separated from the self and incorporated. The land is a collective resource constantly being drawn on in daily life experiences, a collective representation stabilizing the world through the authority of precedence and other selves embodied within it. The identities of individuals are constructed in and through the material remains of ancestral transformations linking them to previous generations and their contemporaries, a world in which every prominent feature is associated with a mythological event. Life-spans are locked into the experience of an ancestral past that binds the universe in a limited topographical space. The narrative of myth is a model of and for social action.

Forests of Eyes, Rivers of Identities

Tanner (1979), in a discussion of religious ideology in relation to hunting practices among the Mistassini Cree Indians of Quebec province, Canada, notes at the beginning of his account that Mistassini is the name of a village and of a band of Indians. The village is situated by a large lake, Lake Mistassini, meaning 'big rock' and referring to a large rock along the western shore of the lake, a name traditionally also used to refer to the Indians inhabiting the region (Tanner 1979: 6). They are thus immediately 'situated' in the landscape and with reference to the details of its topography. Tanner notes that boundaries (notional rather than fixed or absolute) between hunting territories are generally located along high ground or large rivers, and their overall pattern is influenced by travel routes, themselves strongly related to interconnected lake and river systems. Mistassini also refer to their hunting grounds by saying 'my path' or 'my road' or 'my river' (Speck 1932: 460), indicating the temporary social appropriation of terrain *within* a path of movement which may vary from one year to the next. Territory is intimately bound up with life-paths and movements.

Within any particular hunting territory a patchwork of different habitat types exists, each of which favours a particular mix of animal populations. The Cree make great use of their intimate knowledge of the vegetation in planning hunting and trapping. A complex system of classification exists for water bodies according to the type of lake or river bottom, the nature of the banks and shores, the form of the currents and types of vegetation (Tanner 1979: 45). Hunting and trapping require frequent residential change in terms both of types of dwellings and of locales; yet in Cree ideology the illusion is fostered that the place of residence is always the same, and this is effected by a standardized internal

arrangement of domestic space. Whatever the type of dwelling –
log cabin, large dome tent or wooden-framed canvas-covered
tent – it is arranged internally in terms of a rigid division of space
related to gender, age and authority, and family units, so as to
appear to occupy the same space. Whatever the actual camp-site
the Cree, then, are always staying in the same place. Coupled
with this idea of stability despite movement there is a general
reluctance to use old camp-sites in the forest when the group is
hunting. A camp-site should be placed on ground that is clean
and unpolluted by previous occupation, a place that will not be
offensive to the spirits of game animals and other magical entities
that aid hunting. Abandoned camps should be cleaned of refuse,
and they become sacred places. A short time after the camp-site is
left the 'spirit' of the hunting group flies over the place, and if all
is as it should be future hunting success will follow. The doorway, symbolically crucial transition point between the inside and
outside of the winter dwelling, should face both the rising sun
and a body of water. Consequently camps are almost always on
the western shores of lakes. The rising sun is positively valued,
and it is auspicious for the hunter to go out of the doorway facing
the rising sun.

In many rites and myths the dominant conception of space is
framed in terms of a concentric model, with camp space at the
centre surrounded by topographical or physiographical space,
the forests and lakes inhabited by animals, at the farthest reaches
of which and above and below are located spiritual entities
associated with natural forces. A distinction is thus drawn
between inside and outside, and the hunting journey, conceived
as a process of going out, moving in a circle and returning, medi-
ates between the two domains.

Everything in the Mistassini world has a spirit – people,
animals, rocks, clothes, moccasins, tents, doorways of tents and
thus becomes throughly humanized. Spirits reside in anything
that can be *named*, and in a manner akin to that among the
Aborigines the landscape by this means becomes socialized and
populated with spiritual entities and powers, frequently by
associating or linking different ones together. For example,
weather control is an important part of Cree ritual. Winds are
conceived to blow from four different cardinal directions, and
weather is primarily attributed to the actions of the winds and
their spirits. There is also a strong set of beliefs about mountains,

considered to be the dwelling-places of spirits and places where shamans go to practise magic (Tanner 1979: 98). One rite involves a summer-born or winter-born person pointing at a particular mountain in order to bring either warm weather or a snowstorm, respectively.

The Koyukon landscape of north-west interior Alaska, like that of the Cree, is one filled with networks of paths, names and associations. People know every feature of the landscape in minute detail. The lakes, river bends, hills and creeks are named and imbued with personal and cultural meaning. Nelson (1983) points out that the intimacy of the relationship between people and the land is such that it is difficult for a Westerner to either believe or understand. People move in a world that constantly watches – a forest of eyes: 'A person moving through nature – however wild, remote, even desolate the place may be – is never truly alone. The surroundings are aware, sensate, personified. They feel. They can be offended' (Nelson 1983:14). The natural and the supernatural or the mythological are inseparable, so that perception of the natural environment extends from the empirical into the spiritual. Ideology forms a fundamental aspect of day-to-day subsistence activities, and cannot be separated from 'economic' concerns. As with the Cree, all animals, some plants and some inanimate objects such as rocks possess spirits.

Mythologically the world and everything in it was created during the 'Distant Time'. Stories explain the world's origin in a time when animals and natural entities were human. In the Distant Time the landscape acquired its present form. Humans died and were transformed into the animals and plants encountered in the environment and features of the earth such as hills or mountains (Nelson 1983: 16). Relatedness among animals is revealed by Distant Time stories and by observation of specific behavioural characteristics, for example the bones in the head of the sucker fish resemble the objects it stole. A tendency to get along means that animals are relatives. Certain landforms possess a special spiritual power that must be placated or shown deference, and the entire earth's surface is filled with a generalized power, *sinh taala*, essential for shaman's medicine (ibid.: 35). A nebulous but threatening spirit power is associated with many places on the land, bodies of water and mountains. These are places cursed by shamans or have acquired power in a time beyond memory. The entire system of geographical orientation is intimately connected with an intricate web of waterways that simultaneously threaten and sustain life. People orientate them-selves in relation to rivers and river currents (upriver; downriver; toward the water; away from the water; and four prefixes mea-sure distance, for example *dodot*: nearby downriver) rather than in terms of cardinal directions. Relations of distance and nearness are not defined in simple geometrical terms. Rivers are also used to define and sustain social boundaries. Koyukon people identify themselves with reference to river drainages delineating individ-ual or group terms. Despite continuous human activity for mil-lennia the Koyukon impact on the environment has been slight. The only tangible evidence of this long occupation is scattered camp-sites, trails, widely dispersed village clearings, and the overgrown remnants of abandoned locales. The imprint on the land is fundamentally of a cultural character – one of an invest-ment of meaning: 'the flow of land becomes also a flow of the mind ... Almost nothing visible remained to associate [the aban-doned settlement] with humanity. Only the memory of people and events set this place apart from its surroundings and gave it special meaning ... Each living individual is bound into this pat-tern of land and people that extends throughout the terrain and far back across time' (Nelson 1983: 243).

When the Koyukon people cross their land the recollection of events, the recognition of named places and locales, the aware-ness of boundaries, not only invest it with meaning but perpetu-ate the knowledges necessary to locate resources and orientate themselves in space. As with the Aborigines, individual identities and biographies are so closely connected with the landscape that one can act on the other.

Subsistence Cultivators and the Land

Parallel Worlds in Melanesia

> 'You realise that this tree isn't really a tree. It is actually a man, but you and I can't see him because we are only living beings. Our eyes aren't clear. We are not able to see things as they really are'
>   (Informant cited in Harrison 1988: 325).

For subsistence cultivators in Melanesia the relationship with the landscape is no less intimate than among Arctic or Australian hunter–gatherers. Malinowski noted the intimate relationship between myth and the landscape as lived and perceived:

> The mythical world receives its substance in rock and hill, in the changes in land and sea. The pierced sea-passages, the cleft boulders, the petrified human beings, all these bring the mythological world close to the natives, make it tangible and permanent. On the other hand, the story thus powerfully illustrated, re-acts on the landscape, fills it with dramatic happenings, which, fixed there for ever, give it a definite meaning (Malinowski 1922: 330).

More recently, Guidieri and Pellizzi (1981: 13) refer in a general sense to two distinct 'surfaces' of existence in many Melanesian societies. One is fixed, the land of the dead ancestral forces; the other, the land of the living, is mobile, but always gravitating in relation to the first. In this manner in many societies a distinction is drawn between a perceptual order, the plane of everyday existence, and an invisible and underlying order of spirit beings, including totemic ancestors and ghosts of the dead. These spirits are not visible in their real forms, but are 'visible' in metamorphosed transformations in the form of animal and plant species, rivers, mountains and rocks. This hidden order of existence, like the Aboriginal Dreamtime, is atemporal, but constantly intersects with and influences the world of the living. Among the Avatip on the Sepik river in north-west Papua New Guinea to own land is intimately bound up with magical and ritual responsibility for its fertility:

> To the villagers all land and bodies of water are fertile because they contain the rotted bodies and body-fluids of totemic ancestors. Many parcels of land are criss-cross complexes of old levees left by shifts in the course of the river; people say these have human outlines, and still bear the shapes of the ancestors who 'fell down' upon them in mythical times (Harrison 1988: 323).

In this manner the land becomes humanized and socialized as something replete with ancestral energies that requires care and constant sustenance through ritual magic. Beneath the apparent surface of the landscape, but intimately bound up with it, there is a hidden topography best known to (and influenced by) ritual experts in these societies, but emotionally and cognitively pertinent to all. Aspects of the social and ancestral past are both recorded and experienced at specific locales in terms of topographic and physiographic features. Possessing detailed and accurate knowledge of the landscape is bound up with knowledge of intangible worlds and ancestral powers embedded within it, control of which is deemed essential for group production and reproduction.

Whereas in the West there is a tendency to privilege temporal relationships between events in narrative accounts, typically in Melanesia it is spatial relationships that are emphasized. Events are anchored and given significance in terms of particular locales and their interconnections as linked points in space. Particular locales are of essential importance in 'fixing' events and acting as mnemonics, thus creating a sense of social identity and establishing linkages between past and present, the worldly and the supernatural. Küchler (1993) has recently emphasized the point that landscape may act powerfully *as* memory, a template in the process of memory work that is not fixed and static, but something drawn upon in social encounters and disputes over land.

Specific locales in the landscape may be powerful visual reminders of myths and themselves become, through the passage of time, objects of knowledge, the accuracy of which may validate the myths. Landscapes anchor events, and thus act so as to ensure their enduring significance for populations moving around and experiencing them on a daily basis. The landscape provides permanent markers around which life flows and within which meanings become sedimented.

Poole (1986), in a particularly vivid account, discusses this intertwining of a physical and natural and cultural and supernatural ordering of things in relation to the significance of the landscape and the oil that seeps out of it in Bimin-Kuskusmin territory in Highland Papua New Guinea. The Bimin-Kuskusmin live in a rugged mountainous area in West Sepik province. Their territory is bordered to the west by the dramatic Strickland Gorge and on all other sides by formidable mountain ranges. In their mythology the known world is bounded and covered by the canopy of the sky, linked to the earth by massive limestone pillars and trees just beyond the farthest extent of human experience. A mountain chain separates the northern and southern Bimin-Kuskusmin valleys, and this chain is the spine of the land; the seeping oil hidden in a hollow and issuing from a rock crevice is the marrow of the mountain spine. For the Bimin-Kuskusmin the forest is a realm of immense ritual importance and spiritual

power linking the living with the dead and humans with spiritual entities:

> Along limestone ridges and outcroppings the forest growth becomes
> markedly stunted or blighted, and jagged karst formations jut
> through this sparser foliage. Myriad streams, springs, caves, sink-
> holes, rock outcroppings, crevices, cliffs, and other 'natural' features
> of the lower and mid-montaine terrain are identified with ancestral
> events in myths that add sacred contours to the landscape. Lightning-
> scarred trees and places of landslides – all sign's of Afek's [the great
> cassowary, 'mother' of the game animals and father of the sacred
> semen-oil] power – are remembered for the mysterious, 'supernatur-
> al' events that have occurred there. Tiny knolls and forest glades are
> vividly recalled as the sites where a hunter crouched in fear when the
> whistle of a witch, the rumble of an earthquake, or the howl of an
> anquished spirit ... was heard in the vast stillness ... At deep sinkholes
> the spirits of the dead find passage to the ancestral underworld, and
> ancestral spirits return through these passages to haunt and to bless
> this domain (Poole 1986: 175).

The oil was at the centre of all life and ritual practice.
Dedicatory shrines were constructed in a clearing near the oil
seep containing pig, human and cassowary skulls and rock crystals, thought to be animate, sentient and highly sacred. The oil is
carefully collected in a depression encircled by sacred red
Cordyline plants. In an annual cycle of rites ritual experts present
sacrificial morsels of food to the ancestral skulls and the crystals.
The ancestral spirits are then said to return from the underworld
to increase the flow of sacred oil. This central ritual site links
together all Bimin-Kuskusmin, whether living or dead, in a common bond with the land and its resources. The oil represents 'the
source of fertility, growth, renewal and change for all faunae, flo-
rae and humans that dwell on the land ... and even beyond to the
farthest reaches of known human settlement' (Poole 1986: 171).
Only adult men who have undergone the ordeals of a ten-stage
initiation cycle taking place over a decade may approach the
sacred site of the oil. The sacred oil is central to rites of regeneration in which the fertility of the forest is ensured. Oil-soaked taro
is fed to domestic boars, the burying of bamboo tubes of oil is carried out to promote the growth of taro, oil is rubbed on the skin to
make it glisten and ensure personal well-being. Shrines throughout the forest are anointed with oil. The oil is conceived to flow
under the landscape itself in the realm of the spirit world. Proof

and concern (attributed to white infiltration and to the dire ritual consequences of their discovery of the source of the sacred oil) about something's being amiss are areas of unwanted expanding grasslands in parts of Bismin-Kuskusmin territory. In these areas the oil has ceased to flow and the forests have dried up.

For the Foi and the Kaluli of the southern highlands of Papua New Guinea, the relationship with the landscape is no less intimate. They know the course of every body of water, each of which is named. Important landmarks, such as prominent hills, pools in rivers, large trees, are all named and significant places. The naming of places extends to ancestral and more recent events that have taken place. Watercourses provide referents for location and direction: 'the waters, as they turn and fall, generate new localities for every new configuration of land. The name of a locality carries, in effect, its own geographical coordinates, which place it in determinate relation to the brooks and streams that flow through the forest' (Schieffelin 1976: 30). Animals, plants and people are all fundamentally related inasmuch as in origin myths they were all originally human. People have food and shelter by virtue of the plants and animals to which they are simultaneously opposed *and* ancestrally related (ibid.: 95).

Foi territory is characterized by a twofold division: (i) that centrally located and permanently occupied by the longhouse society and its gardens; and (ii) the hunting grounds, *Ayamo*, seasonally occupied for hunting, fishing, trapping and collecting (Weiner 1991: 33). Movement between these two areas was traditionally periodic. *Ayamo* is much larger than Foi gardening territory, and the population disperses in it. Since these areas are occupied at different seasons and are the focus of rhythmic periodic movements, notions of landscape and temporality become interlinked. Changing topography and activities thus have an inbuilt temporal dimension. Creeks and rivers provide major spatial boundaries used to provide a sense of orientation through space and forming the most common borderlines between clan territories. Clan areas are orientated around the mouth and source of identifying streams (ibid.: 40). Distance and nearness, as among the Koyukon, are related to the flow of water. Virtually all place-names have a lexical significance and make use of geographically descriptive words referring to specific topographic features, such as 'creek', 'ridge', 'raised ground', 'grove', 'spur', 'bend in river', 'mountain', 'waterfall'. They also refer to human events and activities at particular locales. The sum of a Foi person's existence is, in essence, the sum of the tracks he or she has made or used during his or her lifetime. A historical consciousness is thus bound up with movement through space. In Foi poetry, Weiner argues, the moving image occurs as a result of the serial juxtaposition of linked place-names and species, which together create a sense of place. By serially listing place-names temporal spans are automatically invoked, and a sense of life movement through a region is constructed. Weiner puts the point particularly well: in showing 'someone else the extent of his land and resource holdings, a Foi man is revealing the fundamental lived dimension of his "Being-there", through the attitudes of care and the actions of concernful appropriation of earthly space, the historical record of the impressions he has made on the land, the inscriptive evidence of his life' (Weiner 1991: 45).

The Foi existential landscape, like that of Australian Aboriginal groups, the Mistassini Cree, the Koyukon and the Kaluli, is doubly imaged, consisting of ancestrally constituted places over which and between which the day-to-day movements of people are transcribed. All these populations key into and draw on ancestral powers. The life path of an individual both iterates an ancestrally created world and creates its own particular and personalized path.

In many areas of Melanesia myth is not only embodied in 'natural' landforms, but also in the form of ancestral stones dotting the landscape (Malinowski 1922; Leenhardt 1930; Riesenfeld 1950; Kahn 1990). Leenhardt records that in New Caledonia 'each stone has a name, a history, a life, we might even say a personality, resulting from the spirit enclosed within it. Often in [remote] valleys I've asked the name for every detail of the land, each notable tree; and the landscape transposes itself into a scheme it would be impossible to transcribe on a map, in which each name is title to a chapter' (Leenhardt 1930: 241, cited in Kahn 1990: 54). Kahn reports that on the coastal mainland of Milne Bay Province stones, some with incised geometric designs, are particularly frequent. They usually represent mythical heroes or heroines who turned into stone, and some of them may play a prominent part in mythological narratives anchoring the stories to the ground. Sometimes the stones may represent the petrification of the personal equipment of the ancestors left behind on journeys (Kahn 1990: 59).

Mountains, Mesas and Tetrads

A number of accounts have emphasized the social and cosmo-logical significance of the land among native American Indian hunter–fisher–gatherers and farmers (e.g. Brody 1981; Hallowell 1955; Harrington 1916; Momaday 1974; Ortiz 1969; Parsons 1939; White 1964). Here I want to refer to one of the richest of these accounts, written by Ortiz, an anthropologist who also comes from the society he studies and interprets, the Tewa, a pueblo-dwelling population engaged primarily in subsistence horticul-ture in the American South-west. Ortiz (1969) describes the Tewa view of existence in terms of six discrete and hierarchical levels or categories of being:

6. Dry food who never did become
5. *Towa é*
4. Dry food who are no longer
3. Made people
2. *Towa é*
1. Dry food people

These are also cultural categories used to divide and classify the entirety of Tewa social and supernatural existence. 'Dry food people' play no official roles in political or ritual life. The *Towa é* make up the core of the political organization of the Tewa. The 'Made people' constitute a hierarchy of eight dis-crete but interrelated organizations, including the members of two moiety societies, the medicine men, the *Kwirana* or 'cold' clowns, the *Kossa* or 'warm' clowns, and the Hunt, Scalp, and Women's societies (Ortiz 1969: 17). The other three categories are supernatural counterparts of the first three. When someone in category 1 dies he or she becomes a spirit of level 4; level 5 represents the spirits of people in category 2; while level 6 is constituted by the souls of the Made people and of all the deities recognized in Tewa mythology before the emergence of humanity.

These social and supernatural categories are superimposed on the landscape in the form of a series of tetrads or groups of four, and related to cardinal directions, topographical features, settle-ment locales, paths of movement and a system of colour classifi-cation (Fig. 2.8). The outer tetrad of the Tewa world is bounded by four sacred mountains, each with unique characteristics. To the north is the Hazy or Shimmering Mountain, to the west the

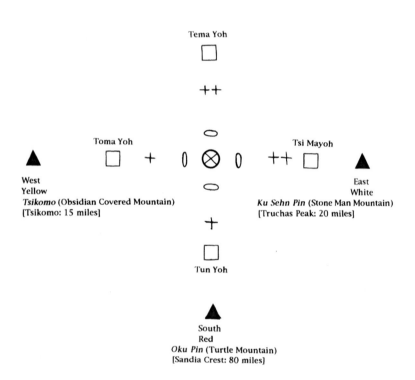

Figure 2.8. Landscape and cosmology in the Tewa world. Based on Ortiz 1969: Fig. 2.

Obsidian-covered Mountain, to the south the Turtle Mountain and to the east the Stone Man Mountain. These mountains vary between 25 and 130 km. in distance from San Juan pueblo, the largest of six surviving villages in New Mexico. All these four sacred mountains can be seen from some reasonably high location in Tewa country. For any particular pueblo the most sacred of them, object of repeated pilgrimages, tends to be the nearest. A lake or pond is associated with each mountain, in which the 'Dry Food People Who Never Did Become', the most sacred supernatural category of beings, dwell linked with the appropriate directional colour. On the top of each mountain there is a *nan sipu* or earth navel, within which the *Towa é* spirits live, watching over the world of the living. This is a keyhole-shaped stone structure in which the bottom end is always kept open and directionally orientated toward one or more of the Tewa villages. It constitutes a point at which the living may communicate with the spirit world. It 'gathers blessings' from the three world levels and directs them through the open end back to the Tewa villages.

A second internal tetrad is constituted by making reference to four sacred *Tsin* , flat-topped hills (mesas) created by the *Towa é* of the directions. These are located approximately midway between the mountains and the village. As they are much closer to the Tewa pueblos they therefore cannot provide, on the ground, a system common to all; and, in practice, different hills constitute cardinal reference points according to the location of any particular village. Each of these hills is sacred because it is believed to be dark and foreboding, and each has a cave or tunnels running through it. These are thought to be inhabited by masked supernatural whippers who are impersonated by the *Towa é*. Unlike the sacred mountains, the *Tsin* are very dangerous places for anyone but the *Towa é* to be, because of the presence of the masked whippers. As with the mountains, the hill closest to any particular pueblo is the most mythologically significant. A third tetrad is made up of the four principal shrines of the directions. These are the most important of numerous shrines found in the landscape around each Tewa village. These shrines are marked by large single stones or collections of stones. These are places in which souls live, and are endowed with sacred qualities. The final inner tetrad is made up of four dance plazas within the village. All public rituals must be performed at least four times on each of these dance areas. In addition there is a 'mother earth navel middle place' within the centre of a village, the most sacred ritual centre of all. Ritual dances and other performances must be initiated here, because it is at the centre of the village. It is circular in shape and, unlike the navels on the sacred mountains, open in all four cardinal directions. Contrasting the two types of navels, Ortiz interprets their relationship in the following manner: 'The mountain earth navels gather in blessings from all around and direct them *inward* toward the village; the mother earth navel is the *source* of all these blessings, so they are directed *outward* in all directions. By the system of ideas at work here, everything good and desirable stays within the Tewa world. This is how relentless and pervasive this tetramerous aspect of Tewa symbolic classification is' (Ortiz 1969: 21–2).

In Tewa cosmology the world is constituted by three levels, that of the middle, mapped out in the landscape as a series of sacred tetrads; the underworld; and the above. These worlds replicate each other, and mediation between them is achieved through the sacred points of the mountain lakes, the earth navels and the shrines. These are points of entrance into other worlds, between a plane of Being and a plane of Becoming. The tops of the mountains are not only points of entry to the world below (conceptually more elaborated in Tewa thought than the upper world) but points at which the upper, middle, and underworlds come closest to intersecting. Their especial holiness is manifested by the presence of concrete signs such as clouds (a source of precious moisture) and evidence of lightning strikes on trees (Ortiz 1969: 25).

From this striking example, considerably simplified from Ortiz's rich ethnography, the significance of landscape as a concretization of a living mythology structuring and ordering the entirety of Tewa social existence and ritual practice could not be clearer. The myths and rituals give meaning to the land and the land itself provides constant tangible evidence of the efficacy and truthfulness of myth as objectified mythology and mythologized objectivity. The landscape provides a concrete means by which the Tewa can understand their world and their place within it. Meaning and order are imposed on the concrete details of the land to answer basic and fundamental questions about the ordering and nature of social existence.

Conclusion

Disregarding all the particular descriptive details, what is clear from all these accounts, whether of hunter–gatherers or subsistence cultivators, is the symbolic, ancestral and temporal significance of the landscape. Writing about an economic 'base' in relation to resource utilization or landscape use seems quite irrelevant here. The landscape is continually being encultured, bringing things into meaning as part of a symbolic process by which human consciousness makes the physical reality of the natural environment into an intelligible and socialized form. The landscape is redolent with past actions, it plays a major role in constituting a sense of history and the past, it is peopled by ancestral and spiritual entities, forms part and parcel of mythological systems, is used in defining social groups and their relationship to resources. Histories, discourses and ideologies are created and re-created through reference to the special affinity people have with an area of land, its topography, waters, rocks, locales, paths and boundaries.

It appears to be evident enough that the significance of landscape for different populations cannot be simply read off from the local 'ecological' characteristics of a 'natural' environment, whether desert, Boreal forest, rain forest or tundra. Nor can it be related in any simple manner to the mode of subsistence (hunter–gatherer/cultivator/mixture of the two) or pattern of dwelling (mobile/sedentary). It, rather, *cross-cuts* these determinisms and distinctions. A much stronger argument can be made that, in all the social contexts I have considered, landscape is intimately related to myth and obeys the same kind of logic as that which structures myth viz metaphor, allegory, synecdoche etc. Landscape is, in substantial part, a mythopoesis and using terms such as hunter-gatherers or subsistence cultivators detracts from rather than clarifies the relationship between peoples and landscapes. What the cases I have discussed share is the selection for myths that stress the conventional and a form of ordering that classically 'resolves' contradictions in social practices.

MYTHOPOEIA : A NARRATIVE GENRE IN WHICH A FICTIONAL / ARTIFICIAL MYTHOLOGY IS CREATED BY THE WRITER.

Part II
Prehistoric Landscapes

Introduction

Human Space and Prehistoric Landscapes

It was something like *that*. I take it as axiomatic that relationships between peoples and landscapes in prehistory were just as intimate and affective as those discussed in Chapter 2. The problem is, of course, to specify exactly in what that *something* might consist. It is neither possible, nor desirable, to try to directly model the significance of prehistoric landscapes explicitly in terms of any of the contemporary examples. We can be sure the situation was different. An examination of the range of modern examples simply provides a conceptual background for attempting to think through the archaeological evidence encountered in the field.

In this and the next three chapters I want to consider evidence from the Mesolithic and Neolithic in south Wales and southern England, attempting to demonstrate both long-term continuities and changes in the relationships between populations and the land. The character of the material evidence to hand is, of course, hardly ideal. For the Mesolithic it consists almost entirely of surface flint scatters representing various temporary and seasonally occupied locales and task-specific sites. Using map grid references to find these sites, there is nothing to be seen on the ground, nothing to indicate that you have even arrived, except, in a few cases, the scars of recent excavations. For the Neolithic settlement evidence is virtually absent, and the primary evidence consists of different types of upstanding monuments in the landscape. Here, at least, you are certain that you have actually arrived and the walk is over.

I have chosen to study three areas in detail: Pembrokeshire, south-west Wales, the Black Mountains area of south-east Wales and Cranborne Chase in southern England (Fig. 3. 0). These have the advantage of possessing Mesolithic find material; and the Neolithic monuments found in each region – portal dolmens and

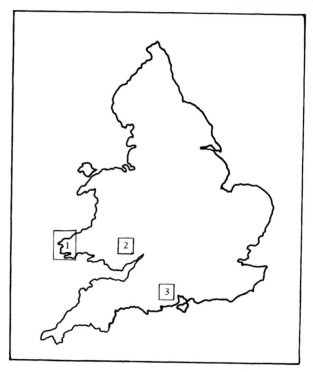

Figure 3.0. Location of the study areas. 1: South-west Wales; 2: The Black Mountains; 3: Cranborne Chase.

chambered monuments, chambered long cairns of 'Cotswold–Severn' type and earthen long barrows, respectively – each represent the main forms found in southern Britain as a whole. The 'natural' landscapes in which these sites and monuments are found contrast dramatically, from the rock-strewn south Wales coastal peninsula to the inland sandstone massif of the Black Mountains to the rolling chalk downland of Dorset. My consideration of the earlier Neolithic in Dorset extends to include two other principal classes of monuments found elsewhere in southern England, but unknown in Wales, the Cursus and a causewayed enclosure complex on Hambledon Hill. My initial intention was to consider the long barrows on Cranborne Chase separately; but, like Richard Bradley before me (in Barrett *et al.* 1991b: 36), I found it quite impossible to discuss them without considering the Cursus. This may in itself be to say something of interest about the *power* of that monument, even when, today, it is scarcely visible on the ground.

Although focusing on landscape the discussions also address the 'problem' of the Mesolithic–Neolithic 'transition', one of the black holes of British prehistory, a chronological drawer in the traditional archaeological filing cabinet that remains almost empty. Previous attempts to discuss the relationship between the final postglacial hunter–fisher–gatherer populations of the Mesolithic and the early Neolithic peoples who, in the received wisdom, began to cultivate and garden, clear the land and keep domesticates, have concentrated on the built environment. The classic example has come not from Britain, but Brittany, where much has been made of adduced structural and depositional similarities between the graves in the Mesolithic cemeteries at Hoëdic and Téviec and early Neolithic long mounds (e.g. Renfrew 1973a: 158; Sherratt 1990; Kirk 1993). Since, in Britain, there is no architectural evidence, and very few Mesolithic burials apart from remains in caves, such a linkage has not been possible to make in these formal terms. Here I attempt to trace instead *process* rather than *product*, the means by which the land became encultured and ultimately transformed into architectural form during the Neolithic, when there arises a need to capture and control what the landscape is about through the medium of architectural morphology.

From a very contemporary perspective, visiting sites in a modern landscape, it is, of course, extremely difficult to attempt to envisage, in the mind's eye, the prehistoric settings of locales. Everything would appear to have changed; at first glance the task seems hopeless. It is simply impossible to know exactly where the trees and bushes were in relation to sites and monuments, where the flowers bloomed and the rushes sighed in the wind. Even the greatest refinements in techniques such as pollen and molluscan analysis can provide only a relatively coarse assessment of these matters, and, concentrating on statistics and counts of oak and lime, arboreal and non-arboreal pollen, they tell us all too little of what the forests and open areas actually looked like and how the plants grew. The skin of the land has gone for good, and can only be partially recovered through the most diligent of scientific analyses; but not its shape. The bones of the land – the mountains, hills, rocks and valleys, escarpments and ridges – have remained substantially the same since the Mesolithic, and can still be observed. Only the coastline has been radically altered. It is the bones of the land and their relationship to sites and monuments with which these archaeological studies are principally concerned.

As a contemporary subject observer interested in interpreting the meanings of prehistoric landscapes I make no claims to an empathetic understanding of their significance, to some incredible feat of being able to find and recover meaning in prehistoric minds. To think *that* is either illusion or to act like God. However, I believe that the experience of place *is* of fundamental significance in the attempt to provide an account. There is one, all too contemporary, experience of place with which most people will be familiar. Locate a monument or site on a map. Drive for hours in a car, and attempt to arrive as close as possible to the place. Walk a shorter or longer distance, if necessary, and you are there. In the case of all but a few well-preserved chambered monuments the result is inevitably disappointing: a few overgrown stones or a low mound covered with rank vegetation in summer is hardly inspiring. You acquire little sense of the feel and character of the land. A monument or place encountered in the course of a walk between places is an altogether different matter. Approaching it slowly, from different directions, and anticipating arriving, it is possible to observe in a much more subtle manner the way in which it is related to its physical surroundings, the lie of the land. Even a site which you cannot see, such as a Mesolithic flint scatter, acquires in this way a greater significance and interest. Even the most dilapidated monument becomes worth visiting. To make the point in a slightly different way, all places are in landscapes, but landscapes constitute the place. Walk from one place to another or approach it from a different direction and everything will change. Things that loomed large in your visual field may become small, or look different. What was at the centre may now be on the periphery; what could be seen has now disappeared, and new horizons have come into view.

This perpetually shifting human visual experience of place and landscape encountered in the walk has not altered since the Mesolithic. Things in front of or behind you, within reach or without, things to the left and right of your body, above and below, these most basic of personal spatial experiences, are shared with prehistoric populations in our common biological humanity. They provide tools with which to think and to work.

Looking at the two-dimensional plane of the modern topographic map with sites and monuments plotted on it, it is quite impossible to envisage the landscape in which these places are embedded. The representation fails, and cannot substitute for being there, being *in place*. Similarly, an unfamiliar landscape remains invisible. You do not know where, or how, to look. This process of observation requires time and a feeling for the place. After being there, after making many visits to the same locales, the intensity of the experience heightens. Monuments that were initially hidden from view on a first visit to a place can now be seen, and patterned relationships between sites and their settings become apparent.

Chapter 3

An Affinity with the Coast: Places and Monuments in South-west Wales

Introduction

The geology of south-west Wales is particularly complex, consisting of a series of sedimentary and igneous rock formations of Pre-Cambrian to Carboniferous age. The landscape has been greatly eroded to create a series of relatively flat surfaces at approximately 60 m. intervals above sea level. Only small areas of the land surface are 200 m. or more above sea level. Despite the fact that this is a relatively low-lying area the coasts and some inland areas display some quite dramatic variations in relief. The greater part of north Pembrokeshire is made up of Ordovician rocks, sandstones, grits and shales broken up by igneous intrusions. These igneous rocks are exposed in narrow strips, and commonly form the numerous headlands along the north-west coast where sheltered bays and inlets have been cut into the softer shales. Inland they form impressive weathered rock outcrops and ridges. Inland in the south of Pembrokeshire the landscape is gentler and more undulating being made up predominantly of Devonian Old Red Sandstone and Carboniferous limestone formations, locally eroded to create low crags and rock outcrops. Along the coast great walls of impressive precipitous cliffs are broken up to form sweeping bays and dramatic headlands.

The coastline of south-west Wales has long generated considerable interest because of the presence of submerged early post-glacial landscapes, exposed within the intertidal zone at very low tides or when storms have eroded away more recent marine sediments. These are made up of peat deposits with fallen tree-trunks and stumps.

Locales in the Earlier and Later Mesolithic

In south-west Wales the Mesolithic evidence almost entirely consists of flint scatters, with a paucity of faunal collections associated with human activities. The surface flint findspots are
remarkably prolific, and have been documented and discussed
by a number of authors (Cantrill 1915; Gordon-Williams 1926;
Grimes 1932; Leach 1913; 1918; 1933; Wainwright 1963; Jacobi
1980; David 1990). They are almost solely confined to the coast for
both earlier and later Mesolithic assemblages. Earlier Mesolithic
flint scatters are concentrated along the south coast of Pembroke,
extending from Caldey island in the south-east to St David's
Head in the north-west. Later Mesolithic sites occur in the same
area, and also extend along the north coast as far east as Newport
(Fig. 3.1). These assemblages vary in size from small, highly localized surface scatters, representing temporary occupations and
resting-places, to quite massive concentrations of microliths,
chipped flint, pebble tools, cores and lithic debris, suggesting frequently visted locales. This material is locally derived from beach
shingles, and does not naturally occur on the cliff-tops bordering
the beaches where the majority of the sites are located.

The dense concentration of the Mesolithic sites along the
southern coast of Pembrokeshire indicates that it was an area that
was extensively exploited throughout the Mesolithic. On the
basis of a survey of 20 sites along the Pembrokeshire coasts from
which there have been substantial lithic collections, as opposed to
isolated finds of one or a few artefacts, five broad types of locale
may be distinguished:

(i) Cave and rock shelters in the faces of limestone cliffs. Four
of these are documented with Mesolithic material, three of which
are on Caldey island.

(ii) Places on flat or undulating rather exposed ground high
up, situated directly on the margins of the cliff-tops and headlands, with extensive views along the coasts and across the sea,
but with restricted visibility inland. The classic case of such a
location is Nab Head, where the site is located on the heavily
eroding neck of the headland, with precipitous cliffs to the north,
west and east. Inland, to the south, the land rises up, and visibility is reduced to a few hundred metres. From the site there are
extensive views across the sea to locales where other Mesolithic
sites are found, to the south and east extending as far as Skomer
island and to the north and west to Ramsey island (Fig. 3.2).

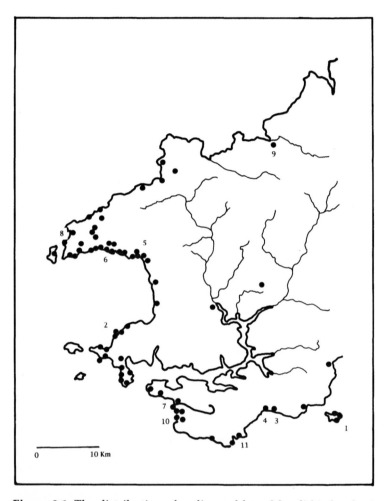

Figure 3.1. The distribution of earlier and later Mesolithic locales in south-west Wales. Places mentioned in the text:

1. Caldey Island
2. Nab Head
3. Manorbier Bay
4. Swanlake Bay
5. Cwm Bach
6. Llanunwas

7. Freshwater West
8. Whitesands Bay
9. Newport
10. Frainslake
11. Freshwater East.

Figure 3.2. Nab Head seen from the north-west.

(iii) Places somewhat withdrawn from the cliff edges, and usually close to springs and streams. The land in most cases rises up gently away from the cliffs, so that visibility inland is restricted to a few hundred metres. From these sites there are more limited views along the coasts, as far as the headlands permit, and visibility across the open sea is restricted. Sites at Manorbier and Swanlake bays, Cwm Bach and Llanunwas are typical of this choice of location.

(iv) Places at short distances from the bases of the cliffs now exposed at low tide, as at Freshwater East (Leach 1913) and Whitesands Bay, sometimes found in association with submerged forests (Fig. 3.3).

(v) Places on flat land or sand-dune areas in river estuary locations or localized marshy areas created by streams. Sites at Newport, Frainslake and Freshwater West (Wainwright 1959) are representative of such locations.

During the earlier Mesolithic sea levels would have been much lower than today, and locales now situated on cliff-tops would have been, at the time of occupation, inland sites situated on the tops of rock outcrops and steep hills overlooking an extensive forested coastal plain. Caldey island, with its caves and rock shelters, would have been linked to the present-day mainland. The cliffs of south Pembrokeshire (Fig. 3.4) would have been the first steep hills and crags encountered inland from the sea, visually dominating a belt of marshy coastal plain broken up topographically by outcrops which now form offshore islands and rocks. The cliffs seen today have been, of course, considerably steepened by marine erosion. Sea levels rose throughout the Mesolithic, crossing modern coastlines and flooding the coastal and estuarine sites located below the cliffs at around 4700 BC. By the early Neolithic the isostatic recovery of the land was greater than eustatic sea level rise, and the relationship between land and sea stabilized (Taylor 1980: 117–19).

Exploitation territories of the later Mesolithic sites would have included tidal strips more substantial than today, inland terrain, extensive marsh areas in some cases, and large areas of open sea, pointing to the significance of marine resources such as fish and seal. Evidence of faunal exploitation is limited to the eroding foreshore peats of Atlantic age exposed by sea erosion around the coasts of Pembrokeshire and mixed cave deposits, indicating exploitation of *Bos*, pig, and red and roe deer (Jacobi 1980: 179–83;

Figure 3.3. Whitesands Bay seen from the chambered tombs at Carn Llidi to the north.

Figure 3.4. View of the south Pembrokeshire coast from St. Govan's Head, looking west.

Caseldine 1990: 40; Lewis 1990). Mollusc exploitation seems to have been limited, although one midden site from Nanna's cave on Caldey island has been claimed (Lacaille and Grimes 1955).

The main regional woodland reflected in pollen diagrams from south-west Wales appears to have been dominated by oak, hazel and alder, with some local pine woodland and alder carr and sedge fen plant communities developing in valley bottoms and low-lying coastal sites (Caseldine 1990; Lewis 1990). At Marros and Abermawr Lewis (1990) attributes increases in hazel counts in pollen diagrams to an opening out of woodlands during the middle Neolithic and the late Mesolithic to early Neolithic respectively. Clearance of the woodland on a large scale, principally by burning, and the creation of a more open 'pastoral' landscape does not seem to have occurred until the middle or later Neolithic onwards. During the earlier Neolithic, when the majority of the chambered monuments were built and used, clearances of the forest were of limited extent (Caseldine 1990; Lewis 1990).

Some writers on the Mesolithic of south-west Wales have stressed the great attractiveness of coastal areas as opposed to inland and upland areas with regard to both possibilities for resource exploitation and the availability of raw materials (Wainwright 1963: 126; ApSimon 1976: 41), while others have pointed to a correlation between the distribution of Mesolithic sites and areas of more frost-free days (Webley 1976: 20–1; Jacobi 1980: 179; David 1990: 251). Important as factors of climate or resource availability may be, the choice of locales on, or beneath, or between, *inland* (in the earlier Mesolithic) or *coastal* (during the late Mesolithic) landmarks – precipitous ridges and rock outcrops that must have been dominant in the local environment – seems highly significant. These, no doubt named, natural topographic features would have been invested with sets of local meanings and would have had the effect of pinpointing the positions of camp sites and their inhabitants to populations moving around in the coastal flatlands or waters and marsh areas surrounding them. The lack of later Mesolithic inland sites may be partially attributable to a lack of intensive survey work, and sites on the higher ground of the Preseli mountains and elsewhere might well be expected; but the evidence that these populations had a special *affinity* with particular (now coastal) locales and areas is overwhelming. The entire area along the coast was extensively exploited. There is, on average, a findspot every four or five hundred metres along some stretches, notably between Angle Bay and Linney Head, south of Milford Haven (Fig. 3.5) and between Porthlyski bay and Newgale sands, with many more yet to be discovered.

Some locales, such as Nab Head (Jacobi 1980; David 1990) and rock shelters on the island of Caldey (Lacaille and Grimes 1955), have clear indications of successive occupation of precisely the same locality from the earlier to the later Mesolithic, despite the fact that local environmental conditions and, consequently, availability of exploitable resources must have changed drastically throughout the Mesolithic. Clearly deciding to stop at a particular place was much more than simply a matter of food acquisition. At Nab Head a series of earlier and later Mesolithic industries have been documented from both surface finds and excavations (Gordon-Williams 1926; David 1990). The location of this site on the neck of a headland, whether we see it today, surrounded by the sea (Fig. 3.2), or envisage it jutting out into a wooded coastal plain, as in the early Mesolithic, is quite striking. The stone-tool industry is particularly extensive. From recent excavations at Nab Head II, dominated by later Mesolithic microliths, over 23,000 pieces of flaked flint and stone were recovered. The assemblage is dominated by backed bladelets, but also includes two pecked and groundstone axes of probable late Mesolithic date (David 1990: 248). Apart from the flint material recovered at Nab Head I a shale 'Venus' figurine was found, and a large quantity (690) of perforated shale beads are recorded both from surface finds and excavation (David 1990: 245). This was clearly a major manufacturing site for these beads. Single finds of shale beads are known from three other sites in Pembrokeshire, and as far away as Waun-Fingen-Felen in the Black Mountains, suggesting either their inclusion in exchange systems between Mesolithic communities or extensive population movements in a seasonal round. It is likely, as David remarks, that a cemetery may once have existed at Nab Head, although there is no trace of it now, and bones are not preserved in the acid soils. The presence of the beads and figurine at Nab Head, its repeated occupancy through thousands of years, and the dramatic location of the site provide us with a tantalizing glimpse of the symbolic dimensions of social Being-in-the-landscape during the Mesolithic, the constitution of biographies in relation to place. As Bradley notes, this period has too frequently been characterized

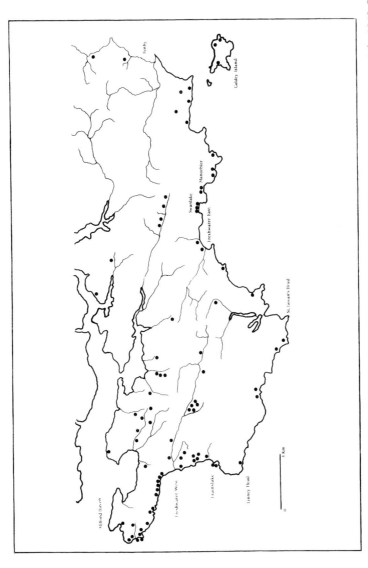

Figure 3.5. The distribution of Mesolithic locales ('chipping floors') south of Milford Haven. After Wainwright 1963: Plate X.

in the archaeological literature as one in which people simply had
ecological relations with hazelnuts, as opposed to social relations
with one another (Bradley 1984: 11).

Proximity to marked changes in relief and jagged rock outcrops was clearly of great symbolic significance during the
Mesolithic in Pembrokeshire, irrespective of the relative positions
of land and sea during the earlier and later Mesolithic. Here it
might be pertinent to note Chase's comments about coastal
Aboriginal populations in Cape York peninsula, northern
Australia:

> Present-day beach people display a high degree of precision in delin-
> eating estate boundaries along the beachline and major rivers.
> Clumps of causarine trees, a rock formation, an intrusive finger of
> dune scrub or a small watercourse provide exact boundary delin-
> eation. Further inland, away from the intensive beach domus zone,
> boundaries are less precise and are conceived in terms of sites or
> unnamed environmental features (Chase 1984: 112).

I want to suggest that it was precisely because the coast provided
both rich economic resources *and* a wealth of named and distinctive natural topographic markers that it was so symbolically
important to both Mesolithic and Neolithic populations. During
the Mesolithic it seems highly likely that settlement locales represent places on paths of movement, bound into the lie of the land
at marked changes of relief with a cosmological significance,
which were ordered sequentially in relation to each other.

The Mesolithic–Neolithic 'Transition'

It is becoming increasingly clear that the terms 'Mesolithic' and
'Neolithic' as a means of characterizing different economies and
social relations of production have outlived their usefulness in
archaeological discourse. The apparent hiatus between the final
Mesolithic and the early Neolithic is a product of these very
terms. All kinds of 'transitions' now seem required to provide
mediations between them (see for example Zvelebil 1986), from
supposedly highly mobile 'simple' hunter–gatherers to 'complex'
settled farmers. It is now generally accepted that Mesolithic communities in Britain and Europe were in no sense less 'complex'
than those in the Neolithic, and the range of variation between

social groups – economic, social and ritual – was equally great (Price and Brown 1985; Gamble 1986). There is no necessary reason to link the building of monuments with the production of an agricultural surplus. And, indeed, it is important to remember that not all surpluses are agricultural. A pastoral surplus which does not require being 'settled' is perfectly possible, and some of the 'classic' surplus societies are, of course, the hunter–fisher–gatherers of the American North-West Coast. From the archaeological evidence there is little to suggest that anything like a fully-fledged mixed farming economy existed in the earlier Neolithic of Britain (Kinnes 1988; Thomas 1991: Chapter 2). Thomas has cogently argued that wild food resources contributed a substantial proportion of food supplies, and that a seasonal cycle of movement lay at the heart of social and subsistence arrangements (1991: 28). I explore the question of an economic 'transition' more fully in Chapter 6.

Monument Construction and the Significance of Place

The coastal location of the Mesolithic sites is repeated in the overall distribution of the chambered monuments of south-west Wales, which in the general absence of domestic sites are the primary evidence for the Neolithic in the area as elsewhere in Britain. The overall distribution of Mesolithic sites and Neolithic burial chambers is *complementary* rather than exclusive. Many of the monuments are situated in exactly the same general areas that must have been habitually exploited during the Mesolithic (Fig. 3. 6). An inspection of the distribution map of Neolithic artefact finds from non-funerary contexts in Wales also reveals that they are particularly densely concentrated in those regions with Mesolithic findspots in Pembrokeshire (Savory 1980). Some specific site locales, such as the Caldey rock shelters, were utilized during both the Mesolithic and the Neolithic (Lacaille and Grimes 1955). Mesolithic locales and artefact findspots also occur in very close proximity to some of the individual chambered monuments, for example those at St David's, Manorbier, Angle, Newport (Carreg Coetan Arthur) and Longhouse (Carreg Samson).

The only Neolithic settlement site known is Clegyr Boia (Fig. 3.7). It may well have been a walled settlement, with

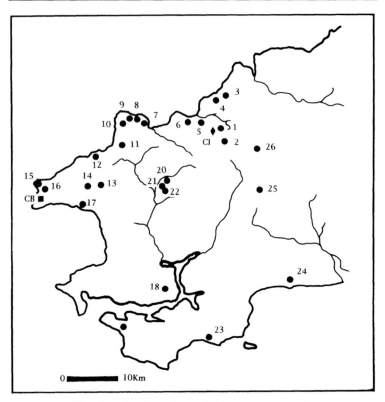

Figure 3.6. The distribution of Neolithic monuments in south-west Wales

1. Pentre Ifan
2. Bedd yr Afanc
3. Llech y Dribedd
4. Trellyffaint
5. Carreg Coetan Arthur
6. Cerrig y Gof
7. Carn Wen
8. Penrhiw
9. Garnwnda
10. Garn Gilfach
11. Ffyst Samson
12. Carreg Samson/Longhouse
13. Treffynnon
14. Tresewig
15. Coetan Arthur (St Davids)
16. Carn Llidi
17. St Elvies
18. Hanging Stone
19. Devil's Quoit
20. Colston
21. Garn Turne
22. Parc y Llyn
23. King's Quoit
24. Morfa Bychan
25. Gwal y Filiast
26. Mountain.

Monuments 1–6: Nevern group. C.I. : Carn Ingli peak; C.B. : Clegyr Boia settlement site.

Figure 3.7. The Neolithic settlement of Clegyr Boia seen from the north-west.

ramparts encircling an area in which remains of two or three Neolithic huts, three hearths and a small midden were recovered (A. Williams 1953: 24 ff.). The excavator thought that the rampart was of Iron Age date because it overlay one of the Neolithic house areas; but the evidence could equally well suggest that there are multiple Neolithic phases present, in which case the site is quite comparable with enclosures from south-west England like Carn Brea and Helman Tor (Mercer 1981). The only identified faunal remains were of cattle. The presence of the midden with limpet shells indicates the continued importance of marine resources in the Neolithic. Importantly, the site is located on the summit of a rock outcrop, 1 km. from the coast, and commanding panoramic views in all directions. It is located less than 3 km. from the nearest burial chambers, situated on the coast to the north of St David's Head and beneath the prominent rock outcrop of Carn Llidi. The positions of these monuments are marked by the rock outcrops below which they are situated. The rock outcrops are prominent from the vantage point of Clegyr Boia, although it is impossible to see the burial chambers themselves (Fig. 3. 8). The major change occurring during the earlier Neolithic would appear not to be of an 'economic' character – there is virtually no evidence that plant or animal domesticates played any prominent role in south-west Wales – but was primarily ideological in nature; and a fundamental part of this changing ideology involved a different relationship between groups and the landscape.

The architectural morphology of the monuments is particularly diverse. This, taken together with the generally poor state of preservation of both the chambers and surrounding cairns and mounds, has defied attempts at classification. They do not fit into any neatly recognizable groups. Rather than considering this as a 'problem' (cf. Grimes 1936a; Lynch 1975), I want to take the line that this is perhaps one of their most characteristic and important features. There are no two identical sites – *difference* is being asserted. It is important that the monuments make a contrasting visual impact. Claims have been made for a significant presence of 'classic' portal dolmens (Lynch 1972, 1975). Such monuments are characterized by the provision of a rectangular chamber with a false high portal entrance fronted by two portal stones with a high blocking slab at right-angles to them. The capstone slopes down to the rear of the chamber, where it is supported by a lower

Figure 3.8. View to Carn Llidi, looking north from the top of Clegyr Boia. The Carn Lidi chambers are situated to the left of the rock outcrop on the skyline.

upright. As Barker points out (1992: 73–6), only one site, Pentre Ifan, can be claimed to match such a description. Others possess sloping capstones, but without convincing evidence of a portal construction. No passage graves with a lengthy entrance passage have been documented. Four monuments do, however, appear to have been provided with very short passages leading to the chamber space (Grimes 1936a: 130–1; Lynch 1976: 75).

This study is based on a survey of 26 separate locations on which one or more burial chambers have been recorded (Fig. 3.6). The total number of monuments is 31, this being a complete sample of all securely documented chambered monuments in Pembrokeshire and the western fringe of Carmarthenshire. All the certain sites identified by Barker in his recent catalogue (1992) are included, and two other monuments, Morfa Bychan C and Treswig, considered by him to be 'probable' sites only. These monuments are all relatively small in size and simple in construction, with the exception of the two largest and most impressive sites, Pentre Ifan and Garn Turne, which possess elaborate entrance facades (Grimes 1936a: 123, 1948). Two unique and unusual sites, Cerrig y Gof and Bedd yr Afanc (Grimes 1939a; Lynch 1972: 81–2), the former with five rectangular cists arranged in a circle in a cairn and the latter a 9 m.-long wedge-shaped gallery construction, are probably late Neolithic in date. Maximum chamber length varies between 1.7 and 4 m. The chambers are usually rectangular or polygonal in form. The capstone, where it survives, is undoubtedly the most visually impressive architectural component of these monuments, and in all cases was almost certainly not originally covered by mound or cairn material. All the monuments with the exception of two or three sites originally possessed only one capstone covering the chamber, and capstone length provides a fairly reliable guide to relative monument size. At least seven of the monuments originally possessed two small chambers. These were originally set in mounds or cairns; but for most sites their ruinous state makes the original shape and size impossible to determine by field survey alone. In three cases there is evidence for the construction of a rectangular cairn; and in a further nine cases the cairn appears to have been originally circular or oval in form. Two cemeteries at Carn Wen and Morfa Bychan, consisting respectively of three and four monuments separated by distances of 70 m. or less, are known. The other monuments are situated at distances ranging between 0.6 and 18 km. from their nearest neighbours (mean: 4.1 km.); but the majority of them are located within a few kilometres of each other.

While the architectural morphology of the monuments seems to involve a stress on difference, their location in relation to topographic features of the landscape is highly structured and repetitive. The relationship to the coastline, especially in relation to bays, inlets and peninsulas, of many of the monuments is obvious, and must have been as important a factor in monument placement as it was for settlements during the Mesolithic. The mean distance from the nearest coastline is only 3.6 km., and 14 of them are situated within 1 km. of the sea, three of which, including the cemeteries at Carn Wen and Morfa Bychan, occur directly in cliff-top locations recalling the exact positions of many Mesolithic locales.

But this relationship to the coast is more complex than a casual glance at the distribution map might imply. Only eight of the monument locations were chosen so that standing by the monument it is possible to *overlook* the sea directly. From 14 sites (54 per cent) the nearest coastline to the monument is visible at various distances away; but there are some striking anomalies. Four monuments are located in such a position that a distant rather than the nearest section of coastline is visible. In the case of the monument at St Elvies, it is located only 300 m. from the nearest coast, yet the sea is completely invisible. Such sites might be described as being coastal, but with an inland visual field. This placement of some of the monuments so that they are hidden from the coastline nearest to them suggests that landscape features other than the coast itself began to play an increasingly important role for monument location during the Neolithic.

One possibility is that the monuments might be located so as to be intervisible with each other, rather than with features of the natural landscape; but, despite the closeness of the location of many of the monuments, intervisibility between them is restricted to a few sites in the northern area of their distribution. Only two of the monuments are sited on the highest points in their immediate vicinity, with extensive views in all cardinal directions. All the others have restricted visibility in one or two directions, with the land rising up immediately beyond the monument, which may be sited on the midpoint of a slope, at the bottom of a slope, or on a relatively high point, with rock outcrops or the land surface rising above it. The monuments, then, were clearly not sited for maximum visibility in the landscape. They were only meant to be seen, or approached, from certain directions.

One notable feature of the peninsulas of south-west Wales is the presence not only of dramatic cliffs but of inland outcrops of igneous and other rocks. Fourteen of the site locations (54 per cent) were chosen in a close or direct relationship to these. A further four sites in the Nevern valley, I will argue, are intimately related to one of the highest and most dramatic craggy outcrops of the Preseli mountains, Carn Ingli, providing a central symbolic focal point for this group of monuments.

Just to the west of Fishguard harbour a north–south row of three stone chambers is located on a high point with originally (the view is now blocked by houses) sweeping vistas over to the east, with Carn Ingli visible in the distance. Immediately to the west of the chambers a rock outcrop juts out and rises above them. These chambers are much ruined; but the capstones and their long axes seem to be orientated so that they face west–east, i.e. towards the harbour below and the rock outcrop above them. This location is duplicated in the only other case in south-west Wales where a row of burial chambers occurs – Morfa Bychan on the south coast. Here there is a north–south row of four burial chambers set high up on a sloping headland next to a long, low and linear rock outcrop blocking all views to the west, and overlooking a small bay to the east (Fig. 3. 9). The chambers here are surrounded by oval or circular cairn structures. These four monuments are situated on a slope rising from south to north, below the outcrop to the west. As one moves up the slope from south to north, the chambers get progressively closer to the outcrop itself, so that the northern chamber is actually built up against it. This monument has an entrance which faces east towards the bay below. In entering the monument from the east one would be approaching and 'entering' the rock outcrop behind it to the west. Moving up the slope from south to north, the third monument is situated directly below a natural stack of rock eroded from the main escarpment, known as the 'Druid's Altar' (Figs. 3.10 and 3.11). This sequence of monuments, progressively situated so as to be closer and closer to the rocks beyond in the course of upward movement, must have been one which was integrated and 'made sense of' through persons moving closer to the rock as they moved from monument to monument. Such a sequence

Figure 3.9. Looking east from the megalithic cemetery at Morfa Bychan to Gilman Point.

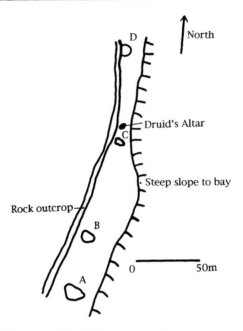

Figure 3.10. Plan of the Morfa Bychan cemetery.

would act so as to connect the monuments systematically to the land as they became increasingly integrated with the parent rock itself.

Built of the same rock as the outcrop itself, and linearly aligned so as to run parallel to it, these monuments are completely invisible from only a short distance away. The rock outcrop itself is clearly visible from Gilman point on the other side of the bay to the east at a distance of 500 m., but not the monuments themselves. The rock outcrops thus simultaneously make the monuments visible and invisible. The natural rocks, such prominent features of the landscape, help to locate the monuments in space; but the monuments themselves cannot be seen.

Such a situation of monument visibility *and* invisibility in relation to rock outcrops is duplicated elsewhere in relation to both coastal and inland monument sites. Two types of rock outcrops were chosen by which to site monuments: (i) 'linear' and (ii) 'circular'. In the first case the monuments, as at Fishguard and Morfa Bychan, are built alongside and against the outcrop, so that the monument entrances in some cases resemble caves in the rock outcrop itself (Fig. 3.12), recalling the caves and rock shelters

Figure 3.11. Looking north from Morfa Bychan cairn B. to the Druid's Altar, below which cairn C. is situated. Note the linear rock outcrop to the left of the Druid's Altar.

Figure 3.12. Garnwnda chamber from the north.

occupied during the Mesolithic on Caldey island. These rock outcrops may be in any cardinal direction in relation to the monument, which can be situated to the west, east, south or north of them; and in one case on St David's Head the burial chamber is located between two low outcrops. In the second case the monuments are constructed at a short distance of no more than a few hundred metres away from a nearby circular outcrop to the west, east or north (Fig. 3.13). Those monuments situated next to the circular outcrops are usually at a greater distance from the coast.

These rock outcrops are clearly dominant focal points in the landscape in a way in which the monuments themselves are not (Fig. 3.14). I have already pointed out that intervisibility is very restricted, even for monuments located at short distances apart. Those located in or near the outcrops are completely invisible until one is next to them. By contrast, the outcrops by which they are located dominate vistas for considerable distances. They are far more visually impressive than the monuments themselves. I will refer to such rock outcrops as natural, non-cultural, or non-domesticated 'megaliths'. The outcrops key the monuments into the landscape, drawing attention to their location and making them special places. At a distance the outcrops indicate where to look for or expect to find a monument. They both mark out monument locations and hide them from the eye. They are all in places up to which one has to climb from surrounding lower areas, suggesting their ritual liminality and removal from day-to-day existence (Fig. 3.15).

These rock outcrops would have served as important landmarks and orientation points, as they do today. Paths of movement might be expected to run between them and the monuments placed by or near to them (Fig. 3.16). For example, the monument at Longhouse, Carreg Samson (Fig. 3.17), is located roughly equidistant between two low circular rock outcrops, with which it is intervisible, one 300 m. to the east and the other to the west, with the coast a short distance away to the north. It is not hard to suggest that these linearly related natural and cultural locales served to act together as symbolically important places on a path of movement along the coast.

None of the Nevern group of monuments (Fig. 3. 6) in the east of the study area are immediately next to or built into rock outcrops, although the largest and most visually impressive of them, Pentre Ifan, is situated about 700 m. to the north-west of an

Figure 3.13. Fyst Samson chamber with 'circular' rock outcrop beyond to the east.

Figure 3.14. Looking north from Ffyst Samson to rock outcrops on skyline. Garn Gilfach burial chamber is built up against the outcrop to the left.

Figure 3.15. Looking south across Manorbier Bay to King's Quoit chamber by the path above the cliffs.

Figure 3.16. Track up to the Carn Llidi chambers built up against the end of the rock outcrop to the left of the photograph.

Figure 3.17. Carreg Samson looking east to 'circular' rock outcrop behind and to the left of the farm.

unusual row of four prominent circular outcrops (Fig. 3.18). It is interesting to note that, while none of the Nevern monuments are intervisible, they are all deliberately sited so as to command vistas of the landscape feature that completely dominates the visual field in this area, the high crag of Carn Ingli. The specific choice to locate some of these structures only a few hundred metres away from their present positions would make this impossible. The largest and most impressive monument in the group, Pentre Ifan, is located directly below Carn Ingli, which is 3.5 km. to the west. There are indications that the original entrance to the burial chamber at Pentre Ifan was on the eastern side (Barker 1992: 24), in which case one's vistas would be completely dominated by Carn Ingli while approaching and before entering the monument chamber. The rock outcrop of Carn Ingli dips roughly along a south to north axis, with the higher end at the south. The dip of the capstone of Pentre Ifan is also south to north, and the ritually important forecourt area is at the higher end. The long axis of the cairn which originally surrounded the chamber (probably built later) also runs from south to north (Fig. 3.19). Here important architectural features of the monument appear to duplicate the incline of the mountain outcrop. From the two northernmost monuments in the group, Llech y Dribedd (Fig. 3.20) and Trellyffaint, there are sweeping views across the Nevern valley to Carn Ingli; but the closest coastline immediately to the north of these monuments, only just over 1 km. to the north, is invisible. Only glimpses of sea, the Fishguard bay area to the west, are visible in the distance. Neither monument is visible from the other. The location of these two monuments seems to have been deliberately chosen with reference to Carn Ingli rather than to the coast, which is only about 1 km. to their north. The relationship of the monuments to Carn Ingli in the Nevern valley seems to be a generalized one, in so far as they are obviously preferentially sited in such a manner that it should be visible from them; and this contrasts with those other cases where monuments are very close to or actually built up against a prominent rock outcrop.

There are only a few monuments whose placement cannot be accounted for in relation to coastal cliffs, crags or rock outcrops; and in these cases the symbolic geography influencing location seems to be highly individualized. Location on natural paths and trackways through the landscape appears to be an important factor here, as might be expected. For example, the monument at

Figure 3.18. Pentre Ifan looking south-west to 'circular' rock outcrops beyond.

Figure 3.19. Pentre Ifan looking west to Carn Ingli.

Figure 3.20. Llech y Dribedd looking south to Carn Ingli.

Mountain is on a saddle of a pass through the Preseli mountains. Gwal y Filiast (Fig. 3.21) is located on a forested slope falling steeply down to the river Taf. Isolated from other monuments and the furthest from the coast (17 km. away), it is situated towards the top of the steep slope running down to the river. The large capstone dips from west to east down towards the river, and the chamber entrance also faces east down the slope. Why *this* location on the river course rather than any other? Standing at the site, the roar of the water below may be heard. Just at the point where the monument is located the river descends with white water down a series of rapids. Upstream and downstream the water is calm. I want to suggest that the monument is located precisely here because of the presence of the rapids below. It is interesting to note in this connection the importance of rapids in rivers in many systems of mythological thought as constituting doors or openings to the underworld.

Conclusion

The finds from excavations of the megaliths of south-west Wales are meagre, even from recent and well-excavated examples (Grimes 1948; Lynch 1975; Barker 1992: 19–21). The acid soils have destroyed all but the remains of cremated human bones, which have been recovered from the chambers of four monuments. The only other finds are a few flint flakes and sherds of between one to three early to middle Neolithic vessels. This does not exactly suggest that the monuments were major foci for artefact deposition. The generally small size of the monument chambers indicates that these were very possibly places for the deposition of a few dedicatory ancestral remains, and were not used for successive interment. Their primary purpose, in fact, seems to have been neither for burial nor deposition. It is difficult to make out a case that they acted as central territorial markers. There is no evidence to suggest that they were marking the centres of areas of land with a high arable component. They rather seem to have acted primarily as symbolic reference and ritually important ceremonial meeting-points on paths of movement, drawing attention to the relationship between local groups and the landscape – itself already a constructed symbolic form of named places, pathways and significant locales from the Mesolithic onwards. I argue in Chapter 6 that the nature of this relationship with the landscape was essentially transformative.

Figure 3.21. Gwal y Filiast from the north-east.

Chapter 4

Escarpments and Spurs: Places and Monuments in the Black Mountains

Introduction

The Black Mountains constitute an upland area of Old Red Sandstone dividing the ancient rocks of mid-Wales from areas of Carboniferous limestone and Millstone Grit to the south. To the north, west and south they rise up to around 700 m. in a series of impressively steep, well-defined escarpments, with spurs jutting into the flood plains through which flow the major rivers, the Usk and the Wye. To the south-east they are irregularly split up by a series of steep-sided valleys cut down by roughly parallel stream systems. A series of chambered long cairns are found in a rough semicircle along the Usk and Wye valleys, the only inland megalithic monuments known in Wales. For south-east Wales as a whole, including the Glamorgan lowlands and uplands, the Brecon Beacons and the Black Mountains area, a series of earlier and later Mesolithic sites have also been documented (Savory 1961; Jacobi 1980: 191 ff.; Berridge 1980; Stanton 1984; Britnell 1984: 136–8; Smith and Cloutman 1988; Wymer 1977). The main concentration of these sites occurs at the head of the Rhondda valleys, and relatively few locales are yet known from central areas of the Brecon Beacons or Black Mountains (Figs. 4.1 and 4.2). This is almost certainly attributable to lack of field survey. The majority of the sites in the Glamorgan uplands were located by field-walking ploughed areas and tracks created by the Forestry Commission from the 1960s onwards.

Mesolithic Locales

On the basis of visits to fifteen locales, from which there are major flint scatters, the following general classes of places may be distinguished:

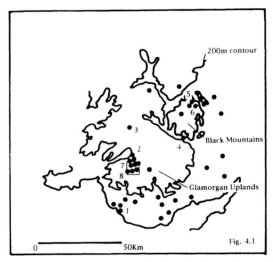

Figure 4.1. The distribution of Mesolithic locales in south-east Wales. For inset see Fig. 4.2. Places mentioned in the text:

1. Ogmore
2. Pant Sychbant
3. Waun-Fingen-Felen
4. Gwernvale

5. Cefn Hill
6. Dorstone
7. Craig y Llyn
8. Mynydd Blaenrhondda.

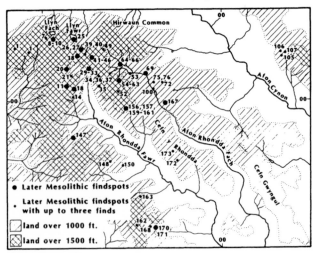

Figure 4.2. Mesolithic locales at the head of the Rhondda valleys.
Source: Stanton 1984: Fig. 12b.
By kind permission of the University of Wales Press

1. Places located in enclosed upland locations around what are now peat bogs but may have been small lakes during the Mesolithic. These occur at the head of small streams which drop down into a major river valley, providing a natural axis for movement through the landscape. Pant Sychbant (Fig. 4.3) and Waun-Fingen-Felen are examples of this type of location. At least twelve flint scatters with earlier and later Mesolithic material have been recovered from the former lake margins at Waun-Fingen-Felen, on the north-east side (Barton, pers. comm.). Just to the south of these flint scatters is a spectacular swallow-hole, surrounded by jagged rocks into which a stream draining the bog disappears.

2. Places located at the bottom of major river valleys on river terraces. There were possibly many such locations, now buried in alluvial deposits. The early and late Mesolithic flint scatter found underneath the chambered long cairn at Gwernvale represents such a location.

3. Places on flat ridge tops by major river valleys, such as Cefn Hill and Dorstone Hill directly overlooking the Golden valley.

4. Places located immediately above dramatic escarpment edges commanding panoramic vistas over the heads of valleys and across passes in the mountains. The extensive flint scatters at Craig y Llyn and Mynydd Blaenrhonnda in the Glamorgan uplands are representative of such locations (Figs. 4. 4 and 4. 5).

Common features of most of these Mesolithic locales are their repeated use from the earlier to the later Mesolithic, a situation chosen to command extensive views in two or more cardinal directions across river valleys, and their positioning on natural routes, trackways or paths through the landscape that would have been followed both by people and migrating animals. Craig y Llyn, for example, is on the junction of natural trackways linking the Glamorgan uplands with those of south Brecknock (Savory 1961: 164). The same general locations appear to have been returned to repeatedly during the earlier and later Mesolithic. While the majority of the microliths from the flint scatters are later Mesolithic in date there is a consistent representation of earlier Mesolithic forms at sites such as Cefn Hill and Waun-Fingen-Felen (Jacobi 1980: 193; Berridge 1980) and Cwm y Fforch in the Glamorgan uplands at the head of the Rhondda valleys (Stanton 1984: 64). At Gwernvale a chambered cairn overlay pre-cairn Neolithic and earlier and later Mesolithic occupation scatters. Half of these Mesolithic sites are located directly below

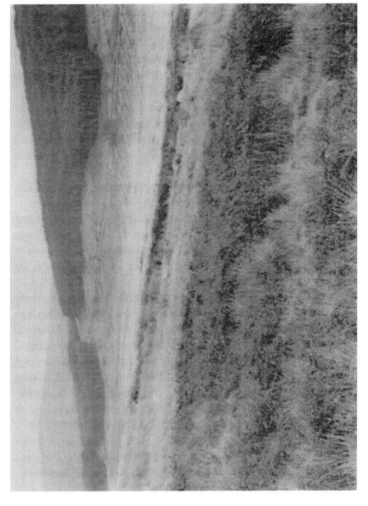

Figure 4.3. Pant Sychbant valley from the north-east.

Figure 4.4. The head of the Rhondda valleys looking south.

Figure 4.5. Craig y Llyn.

rock outcrops or on the tops of sheer escarpment edges – effectively inland versions of the cliff-tops of the Pembrokeshire coast.

Jacobi and Stanton have proposed for south-east Wales as a whole a model of seasonal movement from coastal locations occupied during the winter to upland exploitation camps in the summer similar to that postulated for the Pennines (Mellars 1976), with groups following the upwards migrations of red deer. It is pertinent in this respect to note that the bulk of the flint and chert material recovered from Craig y Llyn in the Glamorgan uplands may be of coastal origin (Jacobi 1980: 195). Recent environmental evidence suggests perhaps the deliberate burning of upland areas to stimulate browse (Cloutman 1983; Smith and Cloutman 1988).

Flint Scatters and Occupational Continuity

Neolithic surface find material is frequently found in the same localities as the Mesolithic flint scatters. There is no positive evidence here of any direct continuity between the Mesolithic and Neolithic; but the choice of precisely the same location for the construction of the Gwernvale chambered monument as had been occupied repeatedly during the Mesolithic suggests strongly something more than mere chance, as Saville has pointed out (1990: 262). One possibility here is that Mesolithic settlement activity continued until the onset of Neolithic settlement beneath the place where the long cairn was later built. The valleys of the Usk and the Wye have long provided routes into and from mid-Wales, providing links with the coastal lowlands of Glamorgan and the Severn and forming a bridge between lowland and highland areas. The site of Gwernvale and its use was embedded in social memory. The fact that this area had been previously settled and cleared of woodland and obstacles, marked by the deposition of cultural debris, a focus for tracks and pathways, suggests a strong symbolic element to the choice of the location, one that could ritually link past and present.

To give some other examples: at Cefn Glas Mesolithic flint and chert artefacts were found just to the south of a Neolithic hut site (Stanton 1984: 59). At Waun-Fingen-Felen activity appears to have continued into the Neolithic, with a charcoal layer at the base of the blanket peat at one site giving a date of 4370–80 BP

(Caseldine 1990: 36). Mixed Mesolithic and Neolithic flint assemblages were recovered from Pant Sychbant and Craig y Llyn in the Black Mountains and the Glamorgan uplands respectively (Savory 1961; Burke 1966; Webley 1976: 31). At the coastal site of Ogmore late Mesolithic material is mixed with Neolithic occupation debris (Webley 1969: 289; Jacobi 1980). Microliths are recorded from the immediate vicinity of Arthur's Stone chambered monument. The repeated utilization of these specific locales, when considered together with a similar overall distribution of chambered monuments and Mesolithic sites in south-east Wales, repeating the pattern already noted for Pembrokeshire, prompts one to infer long-term regularities linking peoples and places. It is tempting to suggest in the light of these observations that Gwernvale may not be an isolated instance, and that many other chambered cairns may be covering locales already utilized during the Mesolithic and embedded in social memory.

Chambered Cairns and the Landscape

The megalithic monuments of the Black Mountains are the only substantial inland group in Wales. At present the location of fourteen monuments is known, and there may originally have been one or two additional sites which have now been totally destroyed (Grimes 1936b; Corcoran 1969: 21–4; Britnell and Savory 1984: 3–9). All these monuments appear to be stone-built long cairns of 'Cotswold–Severn' type. There is considerable diversity in monument morphology. Seven are long mounds with terminal and/or lateral chambers. A few appear to possess additional chambers sealed within the mound, but in the absence of detailed investigation the precise position and nature of the chambers is uncertain in the majority of cases. One site, Arthur's Stone, differs from the rest in that a single elongated polygonal chamber with an anteroom set in an oval mound is approached by an acutely angled passage. All the other cairns possess or would have possessed between two and four or more chambers. Four well-excavated and documented monuments are trapezoidal horned cairns with false portal entrances and forecourts (Grimes 1939b; Savory 1956; Britnell and Savory 1984). Cairn length varies greatly from c.15 m. to c.60 m. The lateral chambers were normally provided with a short passage leading from the edge of the cairn revetment walls. In some cases chambers are paired on opposite sides of the cairn (Fig. 4. 6). For some monuments the chamber nearest to the forecourt was the most massive, suggesting a tapering away of cairn height, which at Pen-y-Wyrlod was at least 3 m. at the portal end (Britnell 1991: 14). Evidence from three excavations suggests that the outer revetment walls of the cairn continued uninterrupted across the ends of the chamber passages (Britnell and Savory 1984: 147), at least in their lower courses. It seems likely that, except during brief periods when access to them was required, the chambers would have been completely concealed in the cairn. At Gwernvale Britnell estimates that lateral chambers 2 and 3 were entered up to at least three times, and chamber 1 at least once, by means of the removal of the revetment wall concealing them (ibid.: 148). The chambers, then, and their entrances were clearly not intended to have a visual impact in contrast with the orientational long axis of the cairn itself (see below).

The cairns of the Black Mountains were built on light Old Red Sandstone glacial drift deposits, with the exception of Gwernvale

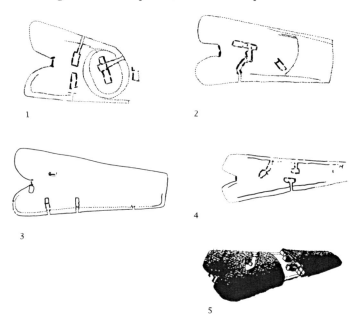

Figure 4.6. Groundplans of selected 'Cotswold–Severn' long cairns in the Black Mountains (not to scale). 1. Ty Isaf; 2: Pipton; 3: Pen-y-Wyrlod, Talgarth; 4: Gwernvale; 5. Reconstruction diagram of Gwernvale.

and Garn Coch, which are situated on alluvial gravels and sands (Webley 1959: 291). Heavy clay soils were avoided, and the principal vegetation surrounding the sites was relatively open dry climax oak forests, with local development of heathlands on the uplands as indicated from pollen analysis from the ancient soil surface beneath the Mynydd Troed cairn (Crampton and Webley 1966). Both Webley (1976) and Savory (1980) have called into question whether there ever was any cultivation in an upland area much better suited to grazing such as the Black Mountains in Wales. Faunal evidence from the Black Mountains is exclusively derived from excavations at the monuments. The presence of the bones of cattle, deer, pig and sheep from the monument chambers and forecourt areas suggests the ritual importance of feasting cycles at the monuments, which were possibly far removed from Neolithic settlement areas.

Webley has argued that the soils, although free-draining, were unsuited to cultivation with a Neolithic technology, and suggested a significant pastoral element in the economy based on cattle and sheep, with perhaps longer- and shorter-distance seasonal transhumance patterns developing between the highland and lowland areas of southern Wales, and more locally between the river valleys and upland areas within the Black Mountains themselves. The cairns are, according to Webley (1976: 30), located within areas that would have been utilized as summer pastures only, with winter settlement occupying the Usk valley and the lowlands of the Welsh coast. The monuments located along the river valleys effectively become markers along pathways from the lowlands to the uplands.

It does not seem necessary to invoke a fully-fledged pastoral economy; but the suggestion that there was a substantial degree of population mobility during the earlier Neolithic, seasonally moving between different landscapes, is pertinent. The overall pattern of social movement, in other words, repeats that already established during the Mesolithic, involving winter–summer, lowland to upland movements. The significant difference would appear to be the substitution of some domesticates, primarily cattle and sheep or goat, for total reliance on wild food resources.

The monuments extend in an arc around the Black Mountains. In the north and west they are located along the valley of the Wye and its tributaries, the Dore and the Llynfi; in the south, along the valley of the Usk and one major tributary, the Rhiangoll. No sites have been documented to the east of the Black Mountains (Fig. 4.7). The monuments are thus located along the major rivers, where the escarpment edge is most regular and clearly defined. From all the monuments except one vistas are dominated by the Black Mountains rising up in the distance. The major rivers or their tributaries are visible from all the sites. From seven of the fourteen monuments the irregular outlines of the Brecon Beacons to the south are also visible in the near or far distance.

The locations of the monuments can be divided into three categories: (i) those situated in a lowland location along the river valleys on or near to river terraces above the flood plain; (ii) in intermediate situations above the river valleys, commanding extensive views but at a relatively low height; and (iii) sites situated high up on ridges and saddles and on undulating terrain below the Black Mountains (Table 4.1). Roughly 50 per cent of the

Table 4.1. Altitudes, orientation and length of the long cairns in the Black Mountains Group. Type refers to altitude – low (L), intermediate (I) and high (H). Map numbers refer to Fig. 4.7.

Name	Map	Height	Type	Ort.	Length
Cross Lodge Farm	1	180	I	W–E	18
Arthur's Stone	2	280	H	NNW–SSE	21
Court Farm, Clyro	3	90	L	NE–SW	32
Pen-yr-Wyrlod, Llanigon	4	251	H	ENE–WSW	15
Little Lodge	5	137	I	N–S	58
Pipton	6	145	L	NE–SW	37
Ffostyll North	7	312	H	E–W	40
Ffostyll South	8	312	H	NE–SW	36
Ty Isaf	9	312	H	N–S	35
Mynydd Troed	10	358	H	NNE–SSW	28
Pen-y-Wyrlod, Talgarth	11	260	H	NNW–ESE	60
Ty Illtyd	12	215	I	N–S	22
Gwernvale	13	79	L	NW–SE	45
Garn Coch	14	19	L	N–S?	19

Figure 4.7. The distribution of long cairns in the Black Mountains. Monument names are given in Table 1. Land over 500 m. hatched.
Relief features mentioned in the text: MT: Mynydd Troed; YD: Y Das; LHK: Lord Hereford's Knob; H.B. Hay Bluff; TM: Table Mountain; HH: Hatterall Hill; ML: Mynydd Llangorse; YG: Y Grib.

monuments are located in the first or second categories and 50 per cent in the third.

Two of the monuments at Ffostyll are situated only about 50 m. apart, the others are situated at a distance of between 2.0 km. and 5.6 km. from their nearest neighbours (mean distance 2.6 km.), thus displaying some considerable regularity in their spacing. Second nearest-neighbour distances range between 2 and 12 km. (mean distance 6 km.). Their location appears to be strongly related to not only the major river valleys but also tributary streams, in such a way that hypothetical 'territorial' demarcation can be related to the flows of river courses (see Fig. 4.7). One of the monuments, Ty Illtyd, is comparatively isolated; the others occur in what may be associated pairs, located in relation to specific landscape features on opposite sides of the major rivers, apart from a small cluster of five monuments in the centre of the distribution.

Orientation and Ritual Axis

The orientations of the long cairns display a complete lack of regularity. All the eight major orientational axes of the compass are represented between the two poles, north to south and west to east. A maximum number of 3–4 monuments share the same orientational axis for the cairn. Cairn orientation differs for all first nearest-neighbours, while only three second nearest-neighbours share the same orientational axis. The most dramatic case of this is the two cairns at Ffostyll situated next to each other, where the northern cairn is orientated W–E and the southern one is almost diametrically opposed, NE–SW. Well-excavated or preserved examples of these cairns do show some regularity in the placement of the broad forecourt area. In the two cases where the cairn is orientated NW–SE the broad end faces SE. For the two out of three documented cases of the cairn running NE–SW the forecourt area faces NE. So, while the orientational axes of the cairns display a complete lack of regularity, there appears to be some uniformity in the siting of the forecourt area in the cases of those cairns sharing the same orientational axis, irrespective of their location in the landscape.

When looked at in the abstract the lack of regularity in the orientation of the cairn axes would seem to suggest that the cairns were orientated at random, that there are no principles regarding their precise directional siting. However, when we begin to consider the relationship between the long axes of the cairns and dominant landscape features an entirely different picture emerges. Two different principles relating to cairn axis orientation may be distinguished:

(i) Cairns orientated with their axes running parallel with the major rivers or their tributaries (five sites); and

(ii) Cairns with their axes orientated towards prominent spurs on the Black Mountains (nine sites).

In the first group the long cairn axis appears to be clearly related to the orientation of the rivers, with the long axis in each case broadly duplicating that of the river valley. These cairns are, as might be expected, all located at low or intermediate heights above the river flood plain (Table 4.1). If one is standing on or at the terminal ends of these cairns one's eye is drawn along the river course, up and down the valley (Fig. 4. 8). The cairn's orientation clearly duplicates that of the river valley. As the river valleys change direction so do the cairn orientations. The only exception to this is the comparatively isolated site of Ty Illtyd, whose cairn axis opposes valley orientation. This site is the only one that could be argued to be symbolically more closely related to the Brecon Beacons than the Black Mountains, and its isolation from the other monuments has already been noted.

In the second group, consisting of cairns in high locations, with one possible exception, for which precise cairn orientation is unknown (Garn Coch), but which is sited within clear view of the spectacular platform of Table Mountain (Fig. 4. 9), the long axis appears to be intimately directionally related to particularly prominent points on the escarpment edges of the Black Mountains-spurs or terminal points (Table 4. 2; Figs. 4. 10–4. 12). Only two of the cairns, Ty Isaf and Mynydd Troed, have both ends of their axes orientated so as to face, or point towards, prominent mountain spurs. One terminal axis of the other cairns faces undulating terrain that either rises up behind the end of the cairn (five cases), thus restricting visibility to a few hundred metres or less, or slopes gently away below the cairn (two cases). The cairns are, in most cases, situated at a distance of between 1 and 6 km. from the spurs to which they are orientated, thus

Figure 4.8. View along the Wye valley to the north of the Pipton long cairn.

Figure 4.9. Looking north from Garn Coch to Table Mountain.

Table 4.2. The directional orientation of the terminal ends of the Black Mountain long cairns in relation to topographically dominant landscape features (spurs and terminal ends of mountain escarpments). See also Fig. 4.7.

Name	Map	End	Points to	End	Points to
Arthur's Stone	2	NNW	–	SSE	Hatterall Hill
Pen-yr-Wyrlod, Llanigon	4	WSW	–	ESE	Cussop Hill
Little Lodge	5	N	–	S	Y Das
Ffostyll North	7	W	–	E	Lord Hereford's Knob
Ffostyll South	8	NE	–	SW	Mynydd Troed
Ty Isaf	9	N	Y Grib	S	Mynydd Troed
Mynydd Troed	10	NNE	Mynydd Troed	SSW	Mynydd Llangorse
Pen-y-Wyrlod, Talgarth	11	NW	–	SE	Mynydd Troed
Garn Coch	14	N?	Table Mountain?		

maximizing the angle of view. In only one case (Mynydd Troed) is the cairn situated directly below the spur, so that one must tilt the head to look up at it (Figs. 4.13 and 4.14).

The cairns on higher ground, then, located away from the main river valleys, connect up with prominent topographic features of the landscape in relation to at least one terminal axis. Despite the fact that they point towards these landscape features, the actual places chosen for cairn location were not themselves particularly visibly dominant high points in the landscape. Only Arthur's Stone, set on a ridge top, commands panoramic views in all directions. Some of the cairns were deliberately sited so as not to be intervisible.

Five monuments in the centre of the distribution of the Black Mountains Group taken as a whole are intervisible, and two others at the south-eastern terminal end (Fig. 4.15). With the exception of Ffostyll north and south, which stand next to each other, intervisibility is restricted between pairs of monuments.

Figure 4.10. Looking south from the end of the Little Lodge long cairn.

Figure 4.11. Ffostyll North long cairn with long axis directed towards spur of Lord Hereford's Knob in the background.

Figure 4.12. Mynydd Troed from the south-east terminal end of Pen-y-Wyrlod, Talgarth long cairn.

Figure 4.13. Looking north from the northern end of the Mynydd Troed long cairn.

Figure 4.14. Looking south from the southern end of the Mynydd Troed long cairn.

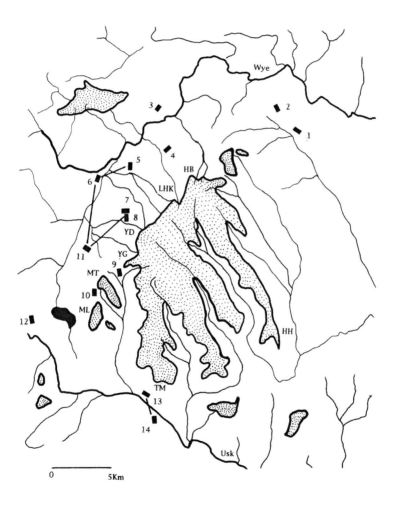

Figure 4.15. Patterns of intervisibility between the long cairns in the Black Mountains.

Clear evidence of siting to prevent intervisibility can be seen in the locations of Court Farm Clyro and Pen-yr-Wyrlod, Llanigon (Fig. 4.15: Nos. 3 and 4). These cairns are situated 3 km. apart on opposite sides of the Wye river. The two sites would have been intervisible had the latter been sited only a few hundred metres to the east of its present location. The view between the monuments is blocked by a spur immediately to the north-west of Pen-yr-Wyrlod, Llanigon jutting out into the Wye valley. The location of the monument seems to have been chosen with precisely this in mind, as were those of others.

The location of the monuments at Ffostyll (see Figs. 4.7 and 4.15: Nos. 7 and 8) in relation to other sites is of particular interest, since this is the only pair of monuments to occur. It is of great interest to note that they are situated exactly in the middle of the Black Mountains Group. Although relatively close to the Pipton and Little Lodge cairns, they are only intervisible with Pen-y-Wyrlod, Talgarth, situated farther away to the south-west. The southern monument has one long axis orientated towards Mynydd Troed (Fig. 4.16), towards which the south-east end of the Pen-y-Wyrlod, Talgarth cairn also faces. The eastern axis of the northern monument faces a prominent spur of the Black Mountains known as Lord Hereford's Knob. The two monuments at Ffostyll are located adjacent to another spur, Y Das, where the line of direction of the escarpment edge of the Black Mountains changes from running in a north-easterly to a south-westerly direction. This change in the angle of direction of the escarpment edge is particularly marked when viewed from the cairn location, but appears less accentuated when looking at a topographic map. The land surface rises gently up to the north and west of the Ffostyll cairns, blocking intervisibility with the Pipton and Little Lodge cairns. However, the southern end of the latter is orientated so as to also face, or point, towards Y Das (Fig. 4.10). A common focal point, in this case, connects together these two monuments, which are not themselves intervisible.

Taking together evidence for monument intervisibility and relationships between monuments and dominant focal points in the landscape to which the cairns are orientated, the Ffostyll cairns, Pen-y-Wyrlod, Pipton and Little Lodge can be argued to form a coherent interconnected sub-group of monuments, including highland and intermediate, spur-orientated and valley-orientated locations. The rest of the Black Mountains Group of

Figure 4.16. Looking south from the end of Ffostyll South long cairn to Mynydd Troed.

monuments form pairs, each of which includes one monument with its cairn orientated along a river valley and the other with a spur orientation (see Fig. 4.7). Thus within each of the five groups monuments align one's vision both along the valleys and towards important dominant focal points in the Black Mountains. The orientation of the mound axes directed and focused attention to the two features of the landscape of essential importance and significance – the Black Mountains and the major valleys running around them. The axes of the long cairns either duplicate those of the natural topography, in the case of those in lowland situations following the orientations of the river valleys, or point towards striking focal points of sacred significance. That these points would have been known and sedimented in social memory from the Mesolithic onwards, and might be associated with ancestral powers, seems very likely.

From 7 (50 per cent) of the cairns, including all those centrally located, the prominent elongated mountain of Mynydd Troed is clearly visible. Two cairns, Ty Isaf and that named after the mountain, flank it, and the largest and most impressive monu-ment in the Black Mountains group, Pen-y-Wyrlod, Talgarth, is located just to the south of it, 1.5 km. away. The long axis of Pen-y-Wyrlod is orientated towards Mynydd Troed, and its high fore-court end is closest to the mountain. It is particularly fascinating to note the similarity in visual form between Mynydd Troed and the original shapes of the long cairns (Fig. 4.17). Could this be why the largest monument in the Black Mountains is built just beneath it, and why it is visible from so many of the monuments clustering in this area?

Looking Out and Going In: Burials, Chambers and Topography

Burial deposits in the Black Mountains cairns have been relatively well preserved. They exhibit features typical for the Neolithic of southern Britain – the differential selection and arrangement of human bones in the chambers, exploiting basic body symmetries such as right and left and upper and lower body parts (Shanks and Tilley 1982; Thomas 1991: Chapter 6). In the Pipton cairn a deposit of bones was discovered under the floor slabs of the south transept in Chamber I, consisting of the crushed skull bones of a juvenile with some added fragments of long bones,

Figure 4.17. Mynydd Troed from the road near to Talgarth.

together with hazel-nut shell fragments and an unworked flint flake. In the chamber entrance there were four other discrete deposits lodged against the sidestones, consisting of a lower-jaw bone, part of a humerus and part of a pelvis and a collection of long bones. Chamber II had seven piles of bones placed against the walls and a further deposit underneath the chamber floor. Lower limb bones are more frequent than upper, and left bones outnumber right in a ratio of roughly 3:1 (Savory 1956: 21–2, 26; West 1956: 47). Chamber I at Ty Isaf contained the remains of at least 17 individuals, with groups of bones positioned along the side slabs and others stuffed into crevices (Grimes 1939b: 126). Smaller quantities of disarticulated remains were discovered in Chambers II and III. The lateral chambers NE II and NE III at Pen-y-Wyrlod, Talgarth contained the disarticulated remains of, respectively, six and seven individuals. Fragments of burnt bone and part of a human temporal bone were also recovered from the socket of a portal orthostat. A child burial in a cist in one of the horns of the monument indicates its secondary use after the monument had been closed and blocked off (Britnell and Savory 1984: 19–23; Luff *et al.* 1984: 36–7).

Apart from the human burial deposits finds from the monuments are meagre. From Pipton the only artefacts recovered were the flint flake from the burial deposit in Chamber I and a sherd of Neolithic pottery from beneath the cairn (Savory 1956: 14–15). Ty Isaf yielded a little more material: two leaf-shaped arrowheads and an axe, a bone pin and sherds from a single bowl in Chamber I, fragments of seven bowls and a sandstone pendant from Chamber II and further Neolithic potsherds from Chamber III (Grimes 1939b: 126 ff.) From Pen-y-Wyrlod, Talgarth only three flint artefacts were recovered, plus part of a bone flute made from a sheep's tibia from Chamber NE III and a few pot fragments, most of which were recovered in the vicinity of Chamber NE III. Of the large number of Neolithic finds recovered from Gwernvale only a few are contemporary with the use of the monument, the rest dating to pre-cairn-construction occupation levels. Finds from the chambers are restricted to fragments of between four and five pots.

Ground plans and the locations of internal monument chambers and passages from excavations or surface survey are known in more or less detail for a number of sites (Table 4.3). Those chambers orientated along the cairn axis obviously share the

Table 4.3. The frequency and orientation of internal chambers in the long cairns of the Black Mountains Group. The frequency of chambers orientated along the cairn axis or laterally/diagonally in relation to it is given. Landscape features noted in relation to moving into and out of the chamber noted: S = mountain spur; U = undulating terrain; EM = middle of an escarpment edge; UN = uncertain orientation of chamber.

Map No.	Freq.	Along Axis	Lateral	UN	IN S	IN U	IN EM	OUT S	OUT U	OUT EM	OUT UN
1	–	–	–	–	–	–	–	–	–	–	–
2	1	1	–	–	1	–	–	1	–	–	–
3	1	–	–	1	–	–	–	–	–	–	–
4	2	1	–	1	1	–	–	–	1	–	1
5	3	–	–	3	–	–	–	–	–	–	–
6	2	1	1	–	1	–	1	–	2	–	–
7	3	2	1	–	–	–	–	–	–	–	3
8	1	1	–	–	–	–	–	–	–	–	1
9	4	–	4	–	1	–	2	1	–	2	1
10	2?	–	–	2	–	–	–	–	–	–	–
11	4	–	3	1	–	–	3	–	3	–	–
12	1	1	–	–	–	–	1	–	1	–	–
13	4	–	4	–	–	–	3	–	–	3	1
14	–	–	–	–	–	–	–	–	–	–	–
Total	28	7	13	8	4	–	10	2	7	5	7

same focal view in the landscape, and it is these that are orientated towards spurs. In other cases the middles of escarpment edges are visible just before entering the chamber. This contrasts with landscape orientation on leaving the chamber. A majority face undulating terrain, others the middle of escarpments. In only one case there is an obvious alignment with an escarpment spur, and this is at Arthur's Stone. Here the passage leading to the chamber bends round at an angle, so that its mouth faces Hay Bluff (Fig. 4.18). This site contrasts with the other Black Mountains monuments in the form and nature of the chamber and passage. While at the other monuments there are good grounds for believing that the internal chambers were sealed and hidden within the cairn, and the entrances to the passages to the lateral chambers only periodically open and visible, Arthur's Stone more probably represents a monument in which the passage may not have been blocked and concealed. Its orientation to a mountain spur as opposed to the lack of orientation of the entrances of the lateral chambers in the other long cairns to visually dominant landscape features then becomes explicable. For the other monuments the orientation of the long axis of the cairn in relation to dramatic landscape features appears to be of great importance, and the chamber orientation of little or secondary significance in this respect. However, what one would see on entering the chamber, largely the middle sections of escarpment edges, appears more crucial than the rather mundane view on exiting facing away from the mountains. But this could also be explained in another manner. Entering the chambers entails removal to a sacred ritual space, which either shares the cairn axis orientation to dominant focal points in the landscape – spurs – or duplicates the orientation of the escarpment edge, thus connecting the chambers with the overall spatial orientation of the mountains themselves. This is particularly important for those cairns whose long axes are aligned along valleys for which we have evidence for chamber orientation (Pipton; Gwernvale). Leaving the chamber entails a return to the domain of everyday life, where an individual would see undulating woodland or pasture. The placement of the bones of the ancestral dead in the chambers in effect sedimented them into the land, and with reference to the orientational axes of the chambers and passages. In this manner the biographies of individuals became fixed in relation to particular places and axes of symbolic significance.

Figure 4.18. Arthur's Stone.

Conclusion

These monuments were clearly not major sites for the deposition of artefacts, as is the case for those in south-west Wales. The successive deposition and subsequent rearrangement of ancestral remains in the chamber was of great significance. The nature of the burial deposits was not purely dedicatory, as may have been the case in the Pembrokeshire monuments. A significant presence of domestic animal bones, sheep, pig and cattle, in the chambers and forecourt areas suggests the use of the monuments in feasting cycles. By contrast with many of the monuments in south-west Wales those of the Black Mountains are monumental, and, in some cases, quite massive constructions, designed to make an indelible and permanent impact on the landscape; and the orientation of the long axis was of the utmost significance. In the Black Mountains there was a *will* to make the monument visible that is not manifested in the same form in many of the monuments in south-west Wales. There the landscape (the rock outcrops) makes the monument visible. In the Black Mountains the reverse seems to be happening: the monuments draw out and emphasize important features of the landscape: the axes of the river valleys and prominent spurs, paths of movement and prominent landmarks whose ancestral significance had already been established during the Mesolithic, and whose meanings were now being re-worked through the process of monument construction, a point further discussed in Chapter 6.

Chapter 5

Ridges, Valleys and Monuments on the Chalk Downland

Introduction

In this chapter I want to consider the relationship between places and monuments in an area of chalk downland in southern England, Cranborne Chase, straddling the county boundaries of Dorset, Hampshire and Wiltshire. While the archaeological landscapes considered in the previous two chapters have often been considered as peripheral to the main areas of early Neolithic settlement, Cranborne Chase has been regarded as one of the most important 'core' areas of Neolithic Wessex in southern England. It is a topographically well-defined chalk plateau bounded to the west by the river Stour, to the north by the Nadder and to the east by the Avon. The northern and western sides have steep and impressive escarpment edges. To the east the dip slope running down to the Avon valley is less sharp and precipitous. The chalk plateau is highest in the north, approaching 300 m., and gently dips down and gradually loses itself in the sandy Dorset coastal heathlands of pine, heather and gorse to the south. From the highest point, Win Green, in the north the Needles and the Isle of Wight can be seen some 50 km. away in the distance on a clear day.

Cranborne Chase is a bold, open landscape in which the lines of the land and its contours are far more significant than its shades, colours and local details. The chalk plateau, roughly rectangular in form and running for roughly 30 km. in a SW–NE direction, is broken up by deep coombes and the Ebble valley in the north. To the south a number of roughly parallel stream and river valleys, the Crichel and Gussage brooks and the headwaters of the rivers Allen and Crane, break up the chalk. This gives rise to a rolling landscape of shallow open valleys separated by gentle rounded ridges around 100 m. high, running NW–SE. Numerous dry valleys lead off the main valleys, giving the local topography of the southern areas of the Chase a more diverse character.

Geologically, the chalk downland is broken up on the surface and alleviated by alluvial deposits along the river and stream courses, Greensand exposures along the western and northern escarpments, and areas with clay with flints in the central part of Cranborne Chase. The highest point in central and southern areas of the Chase is marked by the sandy and gravelly Reading beds which cap Penbury Knoll, crowned today with gnarled pines and visible for up to 12 km. or more across the rolling downland. From Penbury Knoll there are panoramic views across the Chase to Win Green in the north and southwards to the Dorset coast.

Cranborne Chase was, undoubtedly, one of the great ceremonial landscapes of the early Neolithic in Britain. It contains one of the major concentrations of earthen long barrows in southern England, and by far the two most impressive earthworks to be constructed anywhere in Britain during the Neolithic, the 10 km.-long Dorset Cursus and a complex of causewayed enclosures on Hambledon Hill on its western periphery. Field-walking over a twenty-year period has also recovered the largest and best provenanced collection of Mesolithic flintwork from anywhere on the chalk downland of southern Britain.

The Mesolithic Landscape

Virtually all the collections are surface flint scatters. Two small excavations and one more extensive one have been carried out (Catt *et al.* 1980; Lewis and Coleman 1984; Higgs 1959). Field surveys have documented 27 major flint scatters in the central area of Cranborne Chase and in surveyed areas to the north (Arnold *et al.* 1988; Ross 1987) (Fig. 5.1). The overall density of sites is high, ranging between 0.2 and 0.6 sites per square kilometre in surveyed areas. On the basis of the presence/absence of diagnostic microlith types six sites belong to the earlier Mesolithic and two to the later Mesolithic (Arnold *et al.* 1988: 120), while the majority have both earlier and later microlith forms. Taking frequencies of microliths into consideration six sites are dominated by earlier material and ten by later forms.

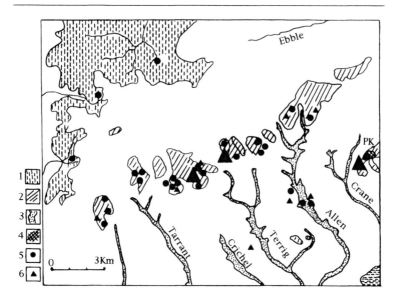

Figure 5.1. The distribution of Mesolithic locales in central areas of Cranborne Chase and finds of early Neolithic leaf-shaped arrowheads in relation to surface geology.
Key: 1: Greensand; 2: Clay-with-flints on chalk; 3: River gravel on chalk; 4: Reading Beds; 5: Mesolithic locales; 6: 1-5 leaf shaped arrowheads; 6: (large symbol) > 5 leaf-shaped arrowheads.
PK: Penbury Knoll. After Arnold *et al.* 1988: Fig. 2 and Barrett *et al.* 1991b: Fig. 2.4.

The fact that most assemblages contain both early and later Mesolithic flintwork points importantly to continuity in the choice of locales and the exploitation and use of particular areas of the landscape. Mesolithic occupation began here perhaps as early as 6,500 BC and continued for 2,000 years or longer, with repeated visits to the same places. Locales on the Greensand, to the north, appear to have been occupied later than those on the river gravels and areas of clay with flints. The spatial distribution of the flint scatters tends to be compact, most sites on the clay with flints covering an area of about 80 by 50 m. Some are considerably larger, one near to Iwerne Minster covering an area of 300 × 200 m., within which smaller, more tightly defined flint concentrations could be identified (Summers 1941). Spreads of material locales found on the Greensand may be up to twice this size (Arnold *et al.* 1988: 122). The flint scatters on the excavated site at Downton situated on a river terrace and dominated by later microlith forms covered an area up to 265 sq. m. (Higgs 1959: 214).

The only structural evidence from these sites is from Downton and St Giles Field, Woodcutts. At Downton a series of 23 stake holes in two discrete areas defining semi-circular or oval areas were identified, together with concentrations of charcoal, worked flints and cooking holes. These may be remains of light shelters with stakes driven into the ground to support them (Higgs 1959: 231). Trial excavations at the Woodcutts site revealed traces of sub-surface digging of Mesolithic date, but the excavated area was too small to provide any basis for an interpretation (Catt *et al.* 1980: 72).

Field visits were made to a sample of twelve of the Mesolithic findspots. Four typical locales can be distinguished in relation to the local topography and geology:

1. Places close to springheads on the Greensand in the north on sloping terrain (*n* = 2);

2. Places on gentle south-facing slopes in undulating terrain on areas characterized by clay with flints in central areas of Cranborne Chase (*n* = 5);

3. Places on alluvial deposits in valley bottoms (*n* = 2);

4. Places on local high points on flat or sloping terrain (*n* = 3).

There is nothing particularly remarkable or distinctive with regard to these places in relation to local topographical features of the landscape, apart from the evidence for substantial Mesolithic occupation and activity on Penbury Knoll/Pentridge Hill, the highest point in the central area of Cranborne Chase (Wymer 1977: 69, 76; Lewis and Coleman 1984). Field-walking and a limited excavation here has recovered a large flint assemblage at a number of separate locations, dominated by early microlith forms, but with a small representation of later types. Of the locales mentioned above, Arnold *et al.* (1988) have noted that the second type (on the clay with flints) is by far the most common, and there is indeed a remarkable degree of preference for areas with rich flint deposits on clay soils.

It is of interest to note that most of the locales are clustered in a broad NE–SW band running across the centre of Cranborne Chase, running from the escarpment edge by Hambledon Hill to the west to Penbury Knoll in the east, with outlying and more isolated site locations on Greensand deposits to the north. This band of Mesolithic sites is clustered between 2 and 4 km. north of the Dorset Cursus and the main concentration of long barrows on Cranborne Chase. They may mark an important axis of movement across the landscape and its alteration through local woodland clearance – an axis which only later, in the early Neolithic, became formalized and culturally embedded by means of monument construction.

Locales and the Mesolithic–Neolithic 'Transition'

Bradley and others (Bradley *et al.* 1984: 89; Bradley in Arnold *et al.* 1988: 125; Barrett *et al.* 1991b: 30) assume that Mesolithic occupation on Cranborne Chase effectively came to an end around 4,000 BC, and that there was a hiatus between Mesolithic occupation and the early Neolithic settlement in which substantial areas of the chalk downland came into use for the first time, as opposed to the preferential occupation of areas with clay with flints during the Mesolithic. Thus, in this scenario, for a period of over 1,000 years Cranborne Chase was unoccupied before the first Neolithic settlement and the construction of long barrows. One possible reason suggested for this is that late Mesolithic settlement shifted from inland to almost exclusively coastal exploitation. Why this should happen remains unexplained. Some sort of gap between the late Mesolithic and early Neolithic remains commonplace in the literature on southern England, but may be more a product of archaeological categorization and the crudeness of relative dating with regard to flint assemblages than anything else. Indeed, Jacobi notes with reference to late Mesolithic settlement in Hampshire that there were 'no obvious areas whose uptake by early farmers will not have impinged in some way upon preexisting patterns of territoriality' (Jacobi 1981: 23). Looking at the overall distribution of Mesolithic and early Neolithic locales in the landscape, continuity rather than a hiatus may be envisaged in relation to both settlement and patterns of exploitation of animal and plant food resources.

The early Neolithic evidence is dominated by ceremonial monuments – earthen long barrows, the causewayed enclosures on Hambledon Hill on the western fringe of Cranborne Chase (Mercer 1980, 1988) and the Dorset Cursus (discussed below). Apart from these sites the only evidence from 'domestic' contexts is the distribution of leaf-shaped arrowheads, one excavated flint assemblage beneath a long barrow (Drew and Piggott 1936), and small ceramic collections from beneath two long barrows and the Dorset Cursus and from settlement pits on Handley Hill closely associated with Wor barrow (Barrett *et al.* 1991b: 30–2). The distribution of leaf-shaped arrowheads, like the Mesolithic flint industries, is strongly related to areas of clay with flints, and there is a concentration of finds on Penbury Knoll. The only change from the Mesolithic pattern is that some findspots now appear on the chalk downland in areas where the long barrows and the Cursus were built. All findspots with over five arrowheads occur in areas already occupied during the Mesolithic (Fig. 5.1). This evidence points not only to the continued use of the same areas of the landscape, but to continuity in economic activities, with hunting, fishing and gathering still playing, as in Wales, a dominant role, supplemented by limited numbers of domesticated animals, the remains of which have been almost exclusively recovered from ritual rather than domestic sites. Moreover, metrical analysis of early Neolithic flint industries has demonstrated technological continuity with the later Mesolithic (Pitts and Jacobi 1979). Gardiner notes that later Mesolithic and early Neolithic flint assemblages may easily be confused in the absence of diagnostic pieces (Gardiner 1984: 19), while Care has demonstrated that the same surface flint sources were exploited for axe production in both the Mesolithic and the Neolithic (Care 1979). Bradley himself notes that Mesolithic activity on Cranborne Chase 'set in motion an oscillation between upland and lowland settlement which was to continue throughout the prehistoric period' (in Barrett *et al.* 1991b: 30). Loess soils, today heavily eroded, appear to have originally mantled the whole of the chalk downland and areas with clay with flints on Cranborne Chase, so that a shift of some Neolithic activity away from areas of clay with flints cannot be explained as a result of a wish to exploit better-quality and more easily tilled soils as part and parcel of a fully-fledged agricultural system (Fisher 1991). Mesolithic activity, as noted by Care, may have substantially affected the forest cover, creating regions of more open country on the chalk down-land attractive to later Neolithic occupation (Care 1979: 100).

Animal bones from earlier Neolithic contexts associated with the Thickthorn Down barrow, and primary silts in the ditch of the Dorset Cursus, include ox, pig, sheep, aurochs, and red and roe deer, with wild and domestic cattle being most frequent (Jackson 1936; Legge 1991). Legge notes the high proportion of wild ani-mals represented by the finds from the Cursus ditch – at least 25 per cent – and that the majority of the remains were whole skulls or parts of skulls, or mandibles, i.e. they do not seem to be ordi-nary butchery deposits (Legge 1991: 55). Cattle remains also dominate the fauna from Hambledon Hill (Mercer 1980: 61). Flotation has also recovered some evidence of wheat and barley cultivation here, on the fringes of the Chase.

Excavations under the Thickthorn Down long barrow at the end of the Cursus revealed a narrow-flake industry of early Neolithic date, together with a leaf-shaped arrowhead and plain bowl sherds (Drew and Piggott 1936; Barrett *et al.* 1991b: 31). As Bradley points out, this probably represents an occupation site over which the barrow was subsequently built. From the old land surface beneath the mound a microlith was recovered, and 'the fact that it was found on and not under the turf-line suggests little differ-ence in age [from the Neolithic flintwork]' (Clark 1936: 91). Since the southern barrow on Thickthorn Down is one of only three totally excavated examples on Cranborne Chase the association between the find of a microlith and an early Neolithic flake industry sealed by later barrow construction is of particular interest.

Excavations on the two major ceremonial monuments of the early Neolithic, Hambledon Hill and the Dorset Cursus, have similarly recovered Mesolithic material. At Hambledon Hill exca-vation of the primary silts of the ditch recovered unspecified arte-facts of Mesolithic date (Farrar 1951: 105–6). Excavations of the west ditch of the Cursus provided two bone samples giving late Mesolithic radiocarbon dates of 4510 and 4950 BC (Barrett *et al.* 1991b: 46); and late Mesolithic occupation of the nearby floor of the river Allen, over which the Cursus crosses, is well attested by flint scatters (Arnold *et al.* 1988; Wymer 1977: 70).

Such evidence can, of course, all be dismissed as purely fortuitous; but at the very least it points to the long-term use and significance of particular locales in the landscape. Undoubtably one of the most symbolically significant of these was Penbury

Knoll, the highest point of the central area of Cranborne Chase, from which there are extensive views in all directions. As has already been noted, concentrations of earlier and later Mesolithic and early Neolithic flintwork occur here. It is of great interest to note that not only does the Dorset Cursus begin due north of Penbury Knoll (see below), but this high point can be seen from no less than 31 of the long barrows (80 per cent) on Cranborne Chase. With one exception those barrows from which Penbury Knoll is not visible occur on the extreme periphery of their overall distribution on Cranborne Chase, and are associated with the escarpment edge defining the area of chalk downland to the north, west and east (see the discussion below). A wish that Penbury Knoll should be visible from the barrows seems to have played a part in deciding where to place them. Shifting some of the barrow sites away from their present locations, sometimes a matter of only a few hundred metres or less, would have made Penbury Knoll invisible. This hill, today capped, as perhaps in the past, by gnarled pines (Fig. 5.2), was undoubtedly steeped in ancestral associations, social memories and myth.

Earthen Long Barrows

There are 39 extant or destroyed earthen long barrows known from Cranborne Chase (Ashbee 1984: Chapter 2; Kinnes 1992: 8–9). They have been well surveyed and documented in the literature (Grinsell 1938–40, 1957, 1959; RCHM 1972, 1975, 1979; Barrett *et al.* 1991b: Chapter 2). Three have been totally or partially excavated and a further five have been subject to antiquarian investigation to a limited extent (Kinnes 1992: 21–3). The barrows exhibit considerable diversity in size, ranging in length from 20 m. to just over 100 m. and from 12 to 30 m. in width (Table 5.1). Some of this variation is the result of differential denudation and destruction. Most would originally have been up to between 3 and 4 m. high at the highest end. One exceptionally long example on Martin Down, which is 150 m. long, may either be a bank barrow or a barrow with an added earthen 'tail' (Barrett *et al.* 1991b: 51). Mound form may be parallel-sided, trapezoidal or oval, but as a result of denudation is often impossible to assess accurately without excavation. Most do appear to have originally been trapezoidal in form, tapering in size from a higher and

Figure 5.2. Penbury Knoll seen from the north-west.

Table 5.1. Morphological characteristics of the long barrows on Cranborne Chase. Map Numbers refer to Fig. 5. 4. Orientation (largest and highest end first), L = maximum recorded length; W = maximum width; D = Ditch type: A, parallel with mound; B, semicircular enclosing one end of barrow; C, completely enclosing barrow.

Barrow Name	Map	Ort.	L	W	D
Pimperne	1	SSE–NNW	106	27	A
Gussage, Parsonage Hill	2	SSE–NNW	26	19	A
Thickthorn Down, North	3	SE–NW	47	20	B
Thickthorn Down, South	4	SE–NW	25	20	B
Thickthorn Farm	5	SSE–NNW	30	18	A
Chettle House (Bar)	6	ENE–WSW	98	20	?
Chettle Wood	7	SE–NW	58	20	?
Gussage South–East	8	ESE–WSW	?	?	?
Gussage Cow Down, South	9	SE–NW	64	14	B
Gussage Cow Down, North	10	SE–NW	50	26	A
Donhead St Mary	11	ENE–WSW	40	18	?
Drive Plantation	12	SE–NW	37	27	?
Wor Barrow	13	SE–NW	45	23	C
Salisbury Plantation	14	NE–SW	43	18	?
Martin Down, South	15	SSE–NNW	102	18	?
Martin Down, Central	16/17	SE–NW	150	21	A
Martin Down, North	18	SE–NW	29	21	A
Martin, Long Barrow Lane	19	SE–NW	40	?	?
Duck's Nest	20	SSE–NNW	44	30	A
Toyd Down, Knap Barrow	21	SE–NW	95	30	A
Toyd Down, Grans Barrow	22	SSE–NNW	58	18	A
Coombe Bissett	23	E–W	51	17	A
Whitsbury Down	24	SSE–NNW	30	19	B
Round Clump	25	SE–NW	72	27	B
Rockbourne Down	26	SSE–NNW	60	27	A
Vernditch Chase, North	27	E–W	23	16	A
Vernditch Chase, South	28	SE–NW	36	24	A
Giant's Grave, Breamore	29	NE–SW	68	26	A
Giant's Grave, New Court Down	30	NNE–SSW	61	15	A
Sutton Down	31	E–W?	23	18	A
Whitesheet Hill, Ansty	32	ENE–WSW	41	23	A
Hambledon Hill, North	33	SSE–NNW	69	15	A
Hambledon Hill, South	34	S–N	26	12	A
Telegraph Clump	35	E–W	96	24	A
Little Down	36	SE–NW	38	24	A
Race Down	37	SE–NW	35	15	?
Tollard, Farnham	38	SE–NW	43	15	?
Pistle Down	39	SE–NW	20	17	?
Furze Down	40	ENE–WSW	56	24	?

broader to a lower and narrower end. The orientation of the barrows tends to be repetitive and standardized. The majority (66 per cent) are orientated either SE–NW or SSE–NNW with the larger and higher end to the south but there are a number of interesting exceptions (Table 5.1). Most originally had continuous or interrupted quarry ditches running parallel to the axis of the mound and flanking it, some with an intermediate berm between the mound and the ditch (Fig. 5. 3).

At least five barrows in the centre of the distribution, closely associated with the Dorset Cursus, have an unusual ditch construction, with the ditches carried around either one, or in the case of one site, Wor Barrow, around both ends of the barrow (Barrett *et al.* 1991b: 32). Two barrows to the east of the Cursus also possess U-shaped ditches (RCHM 1979: xxi)

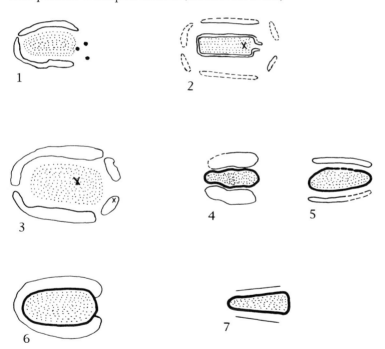

Figure 5.3. Selected groundplans of long barrows on Cranborne Chase. Excavated: 1: Thickthorn Down; 2. Wor Barrow phases 1–2; 3 Wor Barrow phase 3. Unexcavated: 4: Duck's Nest; 5: Grans Barrow, Toyd Down; 6: Round Clump; 7 Furze Down. Not to scale. For orientation and dimensions see Table 5.1. X = position of burials. Extent of mound stippled. After Barrett *et al.* 1991b: Fig. 2.9 and RCHM 1979: Fig. 3.

Of the three reliably excavated barrows on Cranborne Chase, Wor Barrow (Pitt-Rivers 1898; discussion in Kinnes 1992: 22–3 and Barrett *et al.* 1991b: 48–33) is still the most illuminating, with a complex structural sequence, beginning with a long mortuary enclosure with a narrow entrance at the SE end flanked by a post bedding trench, continuing with an embanked mortuary chamber, and ending with an oval-shaped mound with encircling ditches with causeways at the SE and NE ends. The mortuary chamber contained three articulated and three disarticulated (skull and longbone bundles) skeletons, all male. The only artefacts recovered were undecorated early Neolithic pottery and an antler pick in the main barrow ditch. The southern barrow on Thickthorn Down (Drew and Piggott 1936) may have been built successively outwards in bayed sections from the SSE end, defined by rows of hurdles, one running laterally down the mound, the others at right-angles to it (Barrett *et al.* 1991b: 37; Kinnes 1992: 22). It contained no burials, but may have covered a turf 'mortuary structure'. The surrounding ditch is of U-shaped plan, open to the higher SSE end, where a triangular post-hole setting occurred. Early Neolithic bowl sherds were found deposited in the primary silts of the NE ditch segment, and domestic and wild animal bones, including domestic cattle, red deer and wild ox, along virtually the entire length of the flanking ditches, along with deposits of flint-knapping debris. Rescue excavations at Hambledon Hill South recovered only the displaced remains of one adult male inhumation. The ditch segments contained early Neolithic undecorated bowl sherds, a fragment of a stone axe and flintwork (Mercer 1980: 43).

From the sheer size and scale of the barrows and the rather limited numbers of human remains from many excavated examples, both from Cranborne Chase and elsewhere in southern Britain, it is possible that burial of the dead may have been of secondary importance to the experiential impact that they must have had as upstanding monuments on Neolithic populations moving around in the landscape.

The barrows can be broadly subdivided into three main groups: (i) a series of 15 mounds closely associated with the Dorset Cursus and all within 2 km. from it; (ii) a loose western group of seven barrows; and (iii) an eastern group of nine monuments. In addition to these there are eight more isolated barrows on the fringes of Cranborne Chase (Fig. 5.4). The majority of the

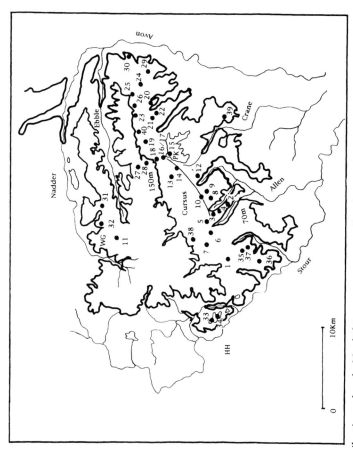

Figure 5.4. The distribution of early Neolithic monuments on Cranborne Chase. HH: Hambledon Hill Causewayed enclosure; WG: Win Green; PK: Penbury Knoll. Long barrow names given in Table 5.1.

barrows occur on their own, but distances to first nearest neighbours are short (mean = 1.5 km.). Three barrow pairs occur, and one cluster of three monuments, all situated at distances of 300 m. or less.

Patterns of Intervisibility

Patterns of intervisibility between the barrows on Cranborne Chase are shown in Fig. 5. 5. These were assessed through multiple visits to every barrow site in clear weather conditions over a period of five weeks. In some cases localized obstructions such as hedges, trees or buildings or later prehistoric earthworks in the immediate vicinity of the barrows meant that these observations had to be taken a short distance away from the barrow site; but this should not unduly affect their reliability. For some sites in or adjacent to dense woodland extrapolations were based on an assessment of the contours of the intermediate terrain. It should be remembered that these are the barrows that are intervisible

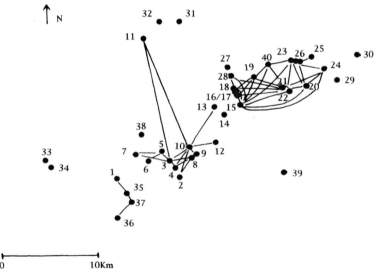

Figure 5.5. Intervisibility between the long barrows on Cranborne Chase.

today in what is for the most part a relatively open and treeless landscape. Judging the precise relationship between the contemporary pattern and the prehistoric situation is difficult, since this crucially depends on the amount of woodland cover. A number of factors indicate that the degree of visibility between barrows during the Neolithic may have been similar or indeed higher than today. It has been argued that the Neolithic environment on the chalk downland of Wiltshire and Dorset was characterized in the earlier Neolithic by woodland clearance and long periods of grassland, possibly maintained by grazing (Evans and Jones 1979). Results of analyses of the molluscan data from three excavations in the central area of Cranborne Chase give a more fine-grained picture. Molluscs from the buried soil surface under the Thickthorn Down South long barrow suggest an open landscape, while those from two sections through the west ditch of the Dorset Cursus 700 m. apart and about 4 km. to the east of the Thickthorn barrow produced contrasting results, one pointing towards an open landscape, the other a rather densely wooded location which remained largely unaltered until the late Neolithic (Entwistle and Bowden 1991). It is worth noting that the samples from the Dorset Cursus ditch are both derived from a low-lying stretch of the monument where it crosses a dry river valley, a damp catchment area of the river Allen. The molluscan evidence may be interpreted as providing a picture of a relatively open upland landscape on the chalk ridges, on which the barrows were constructed, and a highly variable degree of clearance and activity in more low-lying valley locations.

It also needs to be remembered that the present-day intervisibility of the barrows is actively depressed by virtue of thousands of years of denudation and destruction, so that their profiles are lower and more blurred. They are also covered with turf and vegetation, whereas when first constructed they would be gleaming white chalk masses, and, even if sited in woodland, would be likely to be surrounded by substantial clearings. Finally their location on high points must surely indicate a desire that they were meant to be seen from relatively long distances. In sum there is little evidence to suggest that barrows which are prominently sited and intervisible today might not also have been during the period of their initial construction and use.

Intervisibility between the barrows is high in the centre of their distribution, with every barrow being intervisible with one or more barrows in the western, eastern and Cursus groups. Such is the degree of prominence of some barrows that others up to eight or nine km. distant can be seen on the skyline (Fig. 5.5). By contrast, only one of the outlying barrows (Fig. 5.5: No. 11) is intervisible with the barrows in the centre of the overall distribution, and in no other case are the other seven outliers intervisible either with each other or with those in the centre of Cranborne Chase. A clear contrast exists, then, between barrows being intervisible in the centre and invisible on the periphery of their overall distribution. Part of the process of siting barrows in the centre of Cranborne Chase was their relationship to other barrows and the Cursus while, on the periphery, a relationship to topographic features of the landscape, rather than to other monuments, appears to have been of paramount significance.

The barrows may be ranked according to the dominance of their visual field in relation to others. Being able to see other barrows from each mound was clearly an important factor in the location of many of them. In general, it is possible to distinguish between (i) those monuments in which visibility was a primary concern in their location, situated on local high points, false crests and skylines and (ii) those in which visibility was not a dominant concern, situated at lower points in the local terrain. This is a distinction between a local field of monument visibility and a more generalized one. In general terms the closer the barrows are sited to the Cursus the higher their degree of intervisibility. Barrows in the western group are intervisible with between one and three other sites. For some in the Cursus group the numbers of barrows visible from any one site increases dramatically, up to eleven other sites. Those barrows with the highest level of intervisibility with others occur at the terminals of either end of the Cursus on Thickthorn Down (six other sites) and Martin Down, and include the northern barrow on Gussage Cow Down (seven other sites), itself enclosed by the Cursus. The barrow with the highest degree of intervisibility marks the beginning of the Cursus on Martin Down (11 other sites). Barrows in the eastern group have a uniformly high degree of intervisibility, with between four and seven other barrows visible from any one site. The exception is the two long barrows on Toyd Down (Fig. 5.5: Nos. 21 and 22), one or both of which are visible from eleven other sites.

It is of interest to note that those barrows with the highest degree of intervisibility with others form members of pairs of larger barrow groups. In the eastern group the only pair of barrows to occur are those mentioned above on Toyd Down. In the Cursus group pairs or groups of barrows sharing the same alignment are associated with the beginning, end and central stretch of the monument, but only one of the barrows is highly visible, the northernmost barrow on Thickthorn and Gussage Cow Down and the southernmost one on Martin Down. In the western group, where levels of barrow intervisibility are much lower, pairs of barrows do not occur.

One explanation for this pattern might be that sites that were particularly important in the prehistoric landscape and highly visible 'attracted' other barrows through time, and sites built later elsewhere were deliberately sited so as to be intervisible with one or more other barrows. In this manner the construction of barrows on Cranborne Chase gradually created a series of visual pathways and nodal points in the landscape. While some or many barrows are visible from others in the centre of the distribution, comparatively few (30 per cent) are intervisible looking directly down the long axes of the barrows across the landscape. All these cases occur among the barrow pairs/groups associated with the Cursus and the pair on Toyd Down in the eastern group. In all, except the last case, the barrows share the same alignment. Most barrows seem to have been located, therefore, to be seen from the side rather than along their long axes. Looking down the long axes of the barrows the Cursus is visible from 12 sites. Most barrows in the Cursus group channel or 'direct' vision towards this monument, with only a few exceptions.

Many barrows are today located on footpaths, and originally the majority of these mounds may have been located along trackways or natural paths of movement through the landscape. The point at which tracks join may have been emphasized and marked out by a small cluster (2 or 3) of barrows.

The orientation of the long axes of the barrows is closely related to that of the local topography, and in most cases they are aligned so as to run parallel to the contours along ridge axes (Fig. 5.6). In other words, the form of the monument duplicates that of the surrounding landscape in its immediate vicinity. They are situated on high points, with panoramic views in all or three out of four cardinal directions. However, fourteen sites (36 per cent) are situated immediately below rather than on the highest point in the local terrain that surrounds them, with the land rising up and

Figure 5.6. The northern long Barrow on Gussage Cow Down seen from the south-west from the site of the long barrow on Parsonage Hill.

restricting visibility in one or more cardinal directions. Eight of these cases occur in the Cursus group and the other five are isolated barrows on the fringes of the overall distribution. The higher and wider end of these barrows is situated up the slope in these cases (Fig. 5.7). Such an arrangement suggests that the barrows were meant to be seen and approached from a particular direction along a particular path or route, and the siting of those along the Cursus was intimately related to the position of this monument in the landscape. By contrast to the chambered cairns of the Black Mountains, the long axes of the barrows do not direct attention to features of the topography beyond them; they rather form part of that landscape itself. Local differences in the orientation of the barrow axes can generally be explained with reference to the local topography.

In the centre of the distribution in the Cursus group chalk ridges cut up by valleys run NE–SW, an orientation duplicated by many of the barrows. In the western group variations in barrow orientation are closely related to more localized differences in the terrain. For example, the barrow at Chettle Bar is orientated E–W and runs along the top of a small chalk spur that also has an E–W axis. The Drive Plantation barrow (Fig. 5.8) and the Salisbury Plantation barrow in the Cursus group, orientated respectively SE–NW and NE–SW, are similarly aligned along localized ridges. In this respect it is important to note that the barrows fit into the immediate topography of their surroundings rather than being related to a more generalized pattern of the landscape. The orientation of barrow axes was a *localized* decision, and not governed by a more abstract set of rules stipulating how they should be orientated. Those barrows on the margins of the overall distribution are intimately related to the escarpment edges of Cranborne Chase. To the west, those on Hambledon Hill are orientated N–S along the spine of this hill island (Fig. 5.9). Barrows on Sutton Down and Whitesheet Hill are orientated in relation to the escarpment edge. Standing on these barrows looking along their axes an observer's view is directed along the escarpment and towards spurs jutting out from it in a manner somewhat analogous to the situation encountered in the Black Mountains (Fig. 5.10). The same is true of the barrow at New Court Down, whose long axis runs parallel with the contours of the escarpment edge rather than is the case with barrows in the centre of the distribution in relation to a localized ridge. The

Figure 5.7. A barrow on the periphery of the Cranborne Chase group, Donhead St. Mary, near to Ashmore (to the left of the photograph).

Figure 5.8. Track up to the ploughed down Drive Plantation barrow situated with its long axis running along the top of a localized ridge, seen from the north-west.

Figure 5.9. The northern long barrow running along a spine of Hambledon Hill (marked by bushes in the centre of the picture). The ramparts of the Iron Age hillfort are visible to the left.

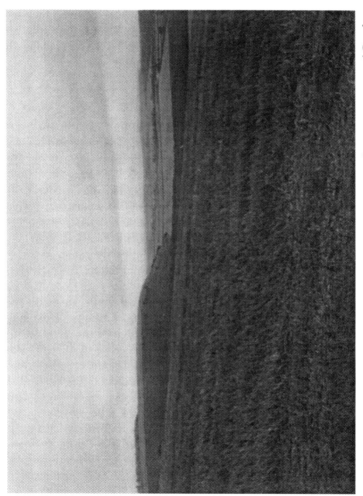

Figure 5.10. View looking west from the barrow at Sutton Down along the northern escarpment of Cranborne Chase.

primary relationship of these barrows, on the margins of the distribution, is to the escarpment edge itself, the break between highland and lowland. Intervisibility with other monuments is not important. What these barrows appear to be doing is to mark out the internal space of Cranborne Chase as significant and special by *ritualizing* and emphasizing its margins. Moving beyond them into the centre of the distribution the local topography of ridge and valley becomes emphasized, with a visual relation between barrows and the Cursus, discussed below.

Hambledon Hill

Two long barrows are associated with another monument complex of different form on Hambledon Hill. Hambledon Hill is a massive clover-leaf-shaped hill set apart from the steep western escarpment edge of Cranborne Chase, with the river Stour flowing close to its western flank and the river Iwerne cutting it off from the chalk plateau to the east. In effect it is a very distinctive 'hill island', a dominant landmark which can be seen from a great distance away to the north, south and west (Mercer 1988: 89). In the liminal space of this island of a hill a massive series of enclosures were constructed, along with the two long barrows, during the earlier Neolithic (Figs. 5.11 and 5.12).

The main enclosure, a rounded triangle in shape, was situated on the crown of Hambledon Hill, consisting of an inner bank surrounded by interrupted ditches. The enclosures on Hambledon Hill bound off interior spaces that are already bounded by the contours of the land. In this manner, cultural islands were created in a topographic space that was already an island. It is likely that this island quality of the place was already understood and appreciated by the Mesolithic populations who visited it and stayed there for longer or shorter periods before venturing up and down the chalk escarpment to the east, demarcating the main mass of Cranborne Chase. During the earlier Neolithic this locale simply became ritualized in a visible form through the construction of the permeable membranes of the causewayed enclosures.

Associated with the main enclosure are mutiple cross-dykes cutting across the spurs of the hill to the west, south and east. Both the cross-dykes and the banks and ditches of the main enclosure were constructed so as to run up to natural breaks of slope on the hill. One barrow was incorporated within this construction,

Figure 5.11. Aerial photograph of Hambledon Hill main causewayed enclosure.   Source: Crawford and Keiller 1923: Plate III.

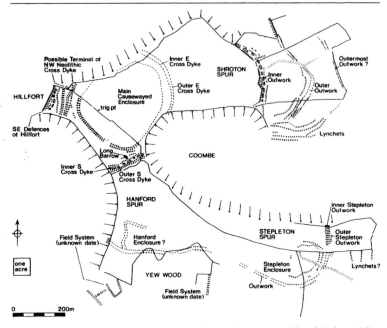

Figure 5.12. Plan of the earlier Neolithic enclosures on Hambledon Hill.
Source: Mercer 1980: Fig. 9.
By kind permission of Edinburgh University Press.

being situated in a not particularly prominent position on sloping land between the southern cross dykes and the main enclosure boundary. The other is set prominently, its long axis running along the spine of the northern spur of Hambledon Hill about 400 m. outside the main enclosure. The main enclosure construction, like the barrows, is clearly related to the contours of the land encircling the domed summit of the hill, while the surrounding cross-dykes cut across the land between precipitous breaks of slope on either side. Although there exists a basic contrast between the bounded circular form of the enclosure and the linearity of the long barrow axis, the placement of the enclosure repeats the close duplicative relationship to natural topography of long barrow location on Cranborne Chase in general, while the linear cross-dykes associated with it cut across the contours of the land in a similar manner to the Dorset Cursus.

Excavation of the interior of the main enclosure revealed the basal segments of around 80 pits (top segments having been destroyed by ploughing). These had been dug into the chalk and partially allowed to silt up; and then a wide range of materials – pottery, stone axes, granite rubbers and antler were deposited in them. A considerable quantity of this material was derived from distant sources – Devon and Cornwall. Some of the pits show signs of recutting and more than one phase of deposition, and the possible erection of posts to mark their positions. The ditch of the main enclosure also revealed careful deposition of materials, but of an altogether different character. In discrete segments of the ditch human bone, animal bone – mainly cattle – pottery and axes had been placed, probably in leather bags. Other deposits consisted of carefully placed human skulls without lower mandibles or associated vertebrae, indicating that they had been placed in the ditch in skeletal condition. After this initial phase of use the ditch silted up, and then was subject to recutting on a number of occasions and further deposition of disarticulated human skeletal material, skull fragments, pottery and flint artefacts. Mercer describes the main enclosure as ' a gigantic necropolis constructed for the exposure of the cadaveric remains of a large population' (Mercer 1980: 63). A minimum of 70 individuals located in the 20 per cent of the main enclosure ditch that was excavated indicates a possible minimum dead population for the site of 350 individuals. The main enclosure was very possibly an exposure area for corpses with associated ritual pit depositions, with some material being taken away and left in the ditches. Hambledon Hill was, in Mercer's words, 'a vast, reeking open cemetery, its silence broken only by the din of crows and ravens' (Mercer 1980: 63).

Sixty per cent of the dead population at Hambledon Hill were children, a proportion contrasting with the relatively few child remains excavated from earthen long barrows in southern England. Many authors have argued for a close association between causewayed enclosures and long barrows in southern England (e.g. Renfrew 1973a,b; Mercer 1980, 1988; Thorpe 1984; Thomas 1991; Edmonds 1993) and that, given the evidence for the disarticulation, differential selection and arrangement of human skeletal material at both the barrows and causewayed enclosures, both played a role in a system involving not only the deposition but also the circulation of ancestral bones. I shall suggest below that these practices may have been intimately related, in a complex ritual cycle, to the third class of monument found on Cranborne Chase, the Dorset Cursus.

The Dorset Cursus

At the time of its initial use the Dorset Cursus was one of the two most spectacular monuments in Neolithic Britain, rivalled in size and the sheer scale of its construction only by the earthworks on Hambledon Hill just 12 km. to the west of its south-west terminal end. The Cursus itself runs for almost 10 km. across the central part of Cranborne Chase from Martin Down in the north-east to Thickthorn Down in the south-west (Figs. 5.13 and 5.14). It consists of two parallel banks with external ditches linked together at the two terminal points with cross banks with external ditches. It is now, for the most part, only visible in the form of soil and crop marks, but sections of it are still well preserved in three places: the south-west terminal in an unploughed field on Thickthorn Down, a section of the south-east bank on Bottlebush Down and traces of both banks in Salisbury Plantation. Aerial photographs

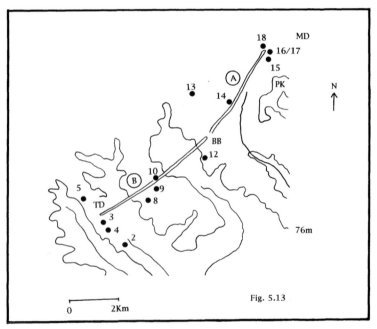

Figure 5.13. The Dorset Cursus and associated long barrows. For barrow names see Table 5.1. MD: Martin Down; BB: Bottlebush Down; TD: Thickthorn Down. A: Pentridge section of the Cursus; B: Gussage section of the Cursus.

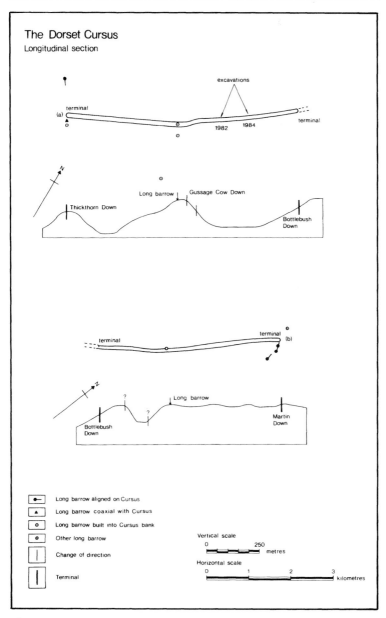

Figure 5.14. Longitudinal profile and plan of the Dorset Cursus.
Source: Barrett *et al.* 1991: Fig. 2.14.
By kind permission of Cambridge University Press

and probing (Atkinson 1955) have verified its course and shown it to have been constructed in two stages, an earlier and longer stretch, the Gussage Cursus, running for 5.6 km. from Bottlebush Down westwards, and a later 4.3 km. stretch, the Pentridge Cursus, continuing from the original north-east terminal onwards to Martin Down. On the basis of probing and excavation (Atkinson 1955; Barrett *et al.* 1991b) the banks appear to have been unbroken by causeways except for gaps near to the Martin Down end. Excavation has shown the ditch to have been steep-sided and flat-bottomed, about 3 m. wide at the top, 2 m. wide at the bottom and 1.2 m.–1.4 m. deep (Barrett *et al.* 1991b: 43). The bank was probably revetted, being located about 1 m. inside the ditch, and parts of the ditch have traces of recutting. Startin (in Barrett *et al.* 1991b: 46) has estimated that the banks may origin-ally have stood at least 1.7 m. high and that the labour invest-ment required to dig the ditch and construct the bank would be somewhere approaching half a million worker-hours. The results of Atkinson's survey and excavations suggest that only one of the ditches of the Cursus maintained a precise alignment, that on the SE side, the NW side having been constructed by means of a series of offsets taken from the SE side; but in sections of the Allen valley at least the NW ditch may have been constructed first (Atkinson 1955: 9; Barrett *et al.* 1991b: 47).

The Cursus is directly associated with at least nine long bar-rows (see Figs. 5.13 and 5.14). Two are incorporated within its course and another seven are directly aligned in relation to its ter-minals or, as is the case on Gussage Cow Down, with a barrow incorporated by it. Of the 39 long barrows which occur on Cranborne Chase the course of the Cursus would have been visi-ble from at least 14 (36 per cent). Penbury Knoll, below which the Cursus starts, is visible from all but eight of the barrows (80 per cent), and two particularly prominent barrows (Gussage Down North and Martin Down South) are intervisible with a large num-ber of barrows from which the course of Cursus itself could not be seen (Fig. 5.5). No less than 22 barrows (57 per cent) are within 5 km. of the Cursus, and only four are over 10 km. distant, on the far fringes of Cranborne Chase to the west, north and east. The course of the Cursus is unique in linking up pairs or groups of barrows situated no more than a few hundred metres apart on Martin Down, Gussage Cow Down and Thickthorn Down. Within the entire Cranborne Chase group of barrows there is only one other site away from the Cursus, Toyd Down, where two long barrows, Knap barrow and Grans barrow, occur very close together at a distance of less than 200 m. Contrasting with the groups of barrows directly associated with the Cursus the long axes of Knap and Grans barrows are not orientated on the same axis but in different directions. The Cursus must have been deliberately constructed so as to link up not only the maximum number of barrows possible but *groups* of barrows. If we attempt to draw imaginary straight lines for an alternative Cursus elsewhere in Cranborne Chase such a situation would not be possible. In no other location in the landscape could so many barrows and barrow pairs be linked together (see Fig. 5.4).

Radiocarbon dates from primary silts in the Cursus ditches indicate that it was constructed around 2,600 BC. Dates from the bottom and primary silts of the ditch of Wor Barrow, just to the north of the Cursus, bracket a time-range of about 2800–2700 BC, and those from other earthen long barrows in southern England generally fall within the time span 2800–2500 BC (Barrett *et al.* 1991b: 51–3; Barrett and Bradley 1991: 9). An exceptionally early date for the southern barrow on Thickthorn Down at the end of the Cursus of 3210 BC may be contaminated and too early. The available absolute dates point to the construction of long barrows before, during and after the construction of the Cursus on Cranborne Chase. The occurrence of precise alignments of long barrows in relation to the Cursus banks at its terminals and the incorporation of two barrows in the Cursus itself (see below) point to a particularly close set of relations between the two classes of monuments, and perhaps a similar ritual and funerary symbolic significance. In the first instance the Cursus linked barrows already in the landscape. Subsequently other barrows were linked to it, an ongoing presenting of the past.

Walking the Cursus

The Pentridge section of the Cursus (Figs. 5.14 and 5.15) begins in the north-east in a relatively flat area of Martin Down. The terminal of the left bank is almost exactly 2 km. due north of the highest point of Penbury Knoll. From the vantage point of Penbury Knoll the entire stretch of the first section of the Cursus is visible, including both the terminals on Martin Down and

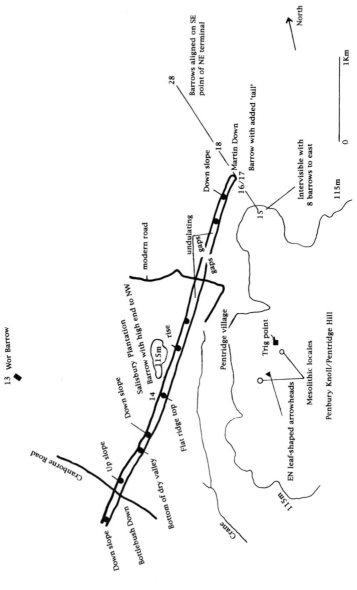

Figure 5.15. Sketch plan of features of the Pentridge section of the Dorset Cursus (discussed in the text).

Bottlebush Down. Parts of the second stretch of the Cursus leading up to the barrow on Gussage Cow Down and the south-west
terminal on Thickthorn Down are also visible from here, but not
intermediate sections of the second half, where the Cursus dips
down into the Gussage and Wyke valleys. From Penbury Knoll a
spur of high ground swings round to the north and dips down,
extending to about 400 m. south of the beginning of the Cursus.
The terminal end of this spur is marked and further emphasized
by a large barrow, today just over 100 m. in length, the second
largest in the entire Cranborne Chase barrow group, only exceed-
ed in length by a few metres by the Pimperne barrow in the
extreme west of the overall distribution. Unusually, this barrow,
rather than following the contours of the immediate topography,
cuts across them – i.e. the direction of the slope of the spur runs
parallel with the long axis of the barrow (Fig. 5.16). Its specific siting makes it highly visible both from the Cursus terminal and
from eight of a group of nine long barrows situated to the east of
the Cursus. Although the Cursus terminal would not be visible
from these barrows this barrow served as a marker for the point
at which it began. The inference that can be drawn from this is
that the group of barrows situated to the east of the Cursus may
be later in date than those associated with its NE terminal end.

The prominent barrow on the arm of Penbury Knoll,
mentioned above, is orientated NNW–SSE, with its higher and
broader end up-slope at the SSE end. The NNW end is exactly
aligned on the NE end of the Cursus and clearly related to it.
About 250 m. due north another massive barrow is sited only
about 10 m. to the south-east of the Cursus end, and again exactly
aligned on its NE end. The mound, 150 m. in length, is by far the
largest in Cranborne Chase (Fig. 5.17). It has been variously interpreted as two conjoined long barrows with continuous side
ditches set end to end (Crawford and Keiller 1928: 232; RCHM
1975) or a bank barrow (Ashbee 1984: 15). Bradley has recently
reinterpreted it as a classic long barrow, its broader end to the
east, with a 'tail' added to, but not continuous with, the eastern
end at a later date, the Cursus blocking possibilities for further
expansion to the north-eastern end, which might otherwise be
expected (Bradley in Barrett *et al.* 1991b: 51). About 250 m. to the
north of the Cursus a smaller, now much ploughed-down,
barrow occurs, aligned again on the north-east terminal, as does
another small barrow in Vernditch wood, 2.4 km to the north.

Figure 5.16. The long barrow (No. 15) on the northern terminal spur of Penbury Knoll.

Figure 5.17. Bank barrow or barrow with 'tail' marking the start of the Pentridge section of the Cursus (No. 16/17)

Penny and Wood (1973: 47) have remarked on the precise geometrical relationship of these four barrows to the Martin Down terminal, one which seems very unlikely to be purely of a fortuitous nature – a point which Bradley has also forcefully made (in Barrett *et al.* 1991b: 51) (see Fig. 5. 15). All these barrows and the Cursus terminal are, or may have been (one is now in a plantation), intervisible, reinforcing their association.

The symbolic importance of the Cursus terminal is thus marked out in the landscape in a particularly effective manner by: (i) a precise relationship with four barrows; (ii) terminating by the largest long barrow on Cranborne Chase; (iii) being situated due north of another massive barrow, intervisible with an exceptionally high number of other barrows to the east, sited on a spur of Penbury Knoll, the highest point and most outstanding natural landmark in the central portion of the Chase, visible from all but a few peripheral barrows in their overall distribution. From this starting-point the Cursus almost immediately begins to dip down gently and swings away from the barrows to the south-west, before following a much more regular course for the next 2.4 km. After less than a few hundred metres the northern terminal would become obscured to an observer walking down the Cursus and looking back to the starting-point. Following this gentle slope the land then becomes undulating, slightly higher to the north of the Cursus, dipping down at first and then rising up steeply to a spur of Penbury Knoll to the south. The Cursus gradually rises up a gentle slope crossing the modern approach road to Pentridge village. A narrow causeway crossed the Cursus on the initial part of this rise, 1 km. from the Martin Down terminus, the only one documented for the entire length of the first stretch of the Cursus (Atkinson 1955: 8), affording uninterrupted views towards Penbury Knoll through the Cursus banks to the south and across rolling downland to the north. This would probably be the last point at which an individual, walking down inside the possibly 1.7 m. high Cursus banks, would be able to have an extensive view of the landscape beyond and outside it to the left (south) or the right (north).

The initial 3 km. stretch of the Cursus running towards Bottlebush Down follows a course that runs parallel to an arm of Penbury Knoll extending as far west and south as the upper reaches of the Crane valley (Fig. 5.18). This provides the dominant focal viewpoint to the south, and the ridge top would be

Figure 5.18. View toward Penbury Knoll from a position just to the south of the Cursus by Salisbury Plantation in the Pentridge section.

visible on the skyline beyond the left Cursus bank. To the north the land is gentle and undulating, and nothing would be visible beyond the right-hand bank of the Cursus to those moving along within. Beyond the modern approach road to Pentridge the Cursus crosses a 350 m. stretch of relatively flat land constituting a localized high point, the land dipping away at first to the south, and then rising up towards Penbury Knoll. It then gradually rises up for another 750 m., crossing two shallow dips to another localized high point, a flat ridge top, now covered by Salisbury plantation, which extends for about 400 m. In the centre of this flat area the first monument along the course of the Cursus, in the right-hand or northern bank, is encountered. This is a long barrow, orientated NE–SW, of medium size, 43 m. long, 18 m. wide and now 2.4 m. high at the NE end, tapering off to the south-west. This barrow orientation is highly unusual for the Cranborne Chase group of barrows taken as a whole, and is only shared by one other barrow on the extreme periphery of the overall distribution to the east, the Giant's Grave, Breamore. The barrow is clearly orientated to run parallel to the contours of the ridge top, which is the case for many others in the Cranborne Chase group; but its orientation is precisely the *reverse* of the norm, SE–NW, with the broader and higher end to the SE. To any observer familiar with the usual orientation of long barrows and the placement of the higher forecourt end, this would constitute a striking surprise and contrast. In comparative visual effect to the barrows at the beginning of the Dorset Cursus, this is the world *reversed*. Another point of significance is that the barrow is incorporated in the right-hand or north-west bank of the Cursus, whereas all the emphasis on alignments of the barrows at the Martin Down terminal was on the left-hand or south-east terminal point, another contrast and reversal.

Field survey (Atkinson 1955: 7; RCHM 1975) has shown that the north-west bank of the Cursus runs up to and is aligned on the barrow at both ends, but that the long axis of the barrow differs from that of the Cursus banks by about 10 degrees. Atkinson's inference is that the Cursus was constructed so as to be aligned on a previously existing barrow. Bradley makes the suggestion that because the alignments are not precise this barrow might have been built alongside an early (marking out?) phase of the construction of the Cursus, and only incorporated into the bank when the earthwork was enlarged (Bradley in

Barrett *et al.* 1991b: 49). Whether this barrow predates, postdates or is contemporary with the construction of the Cursus cannot be established without excavation. Whatever the precise chronological relationship, the lack of precise incorporation into the Cursus bank is of considerable symbolic significance. This was *intended* to be the case: the monument should be both incorporated into the Cursus banks and maintain its identity and visual impact by being differentiated from them. One means of differentiation was the difference in height and width of the barrow from the Cursus banks, particularly marked at the higher NW end, the other the slight difference in orientation. Walking down the Cursus the barrow would only be visible to an observer approaching it from a short distance away – a matter of no more than 100 m. Encountering it would constitute a surprise, and the greatest visual impact on an observer would be for someone moving south-west from the Martin Down terminal in the north-east.

The barrow is situated approximately two-thirds the distance (2.6 km.) along the first stretch of the Cursus, and from it neither the terminus on Martin Down, with its associated barrows, nor that on Bottlebush Down are visible. The only other barrow that might have been visible, and this only if an observer stood on top of the barrow looking out, would be Wor barrow, situated 1.3 km. on the skyline to the north-west (the view is now blocked by a plantation).

A few hundred metres beyond the barrow the Cursus begins to dip down, at first gently, and then very steeply into a dry valley. Today the valley is cut along its bottom by a deep drainage ditch, which is water-filled in winter. At the time of the construction and use of the Cursus the valley bottom would have been boggy land, and water-filled for much of the year. This valley is, without doubt, the most dramatic, steep-sided, change of relief along the entire length of both sections of the Cursus (Fig. 5.19). It also marks the point at which the familiar landmark of the arm of Penbury Knoll to the south of the Cursus tapers away and disappears. Walking down into the boggy depths of this valley provides a sensation of the entire world being removed. Views along the valley itself would be blocked by the Cursus banks, that behind and in front by the steep slopes of the terrain. The top of Penbury Knoll itself becomes invisible for the first time, and with it, the familiarity and reassurance of a well-known landmark, steeped in ancestral associations going back to the Mesolithic, is lost.

Figure 5.19. Looking south-west along the Pentridge section of the Cursus down the dry valley and up to Bottlebush Down.

Up to this point the first section of the Cursus traverses only very gently undulating terrain, the differences in relief being slight, and the Cursus axis itself parallels and follows the axis of the high ground of Penbury Knoll, meeting its northern, and following its southern ridged spurs. The Cursus is keyed into and follows the line of the high ground running to the south of its south-western bank. The relationship of the axis of the cultural monument to that established by the natural topography is one of imitation or duplication. The Cursus is sited at a distance varying between 200 and 500 m. from the point at which the much higher ground of the upper parts of the ridges of Penbury Knoll rise up on its southern side. It is thus situated at an appropriate distance away to maximize the visual impact of the change of relief and also to afford a comfortable angle of view over the top of the Cursus banks (depending on their exact height), which are not too close and not too far away. The Cursus itself is dovetailed into the contours of the immediate landscape surrounding it to the north and the south as if forming a natural and integral part of it. Crossing this first very steep-sided valley that relationship now dramatically changes to one of contrast or contradiction. Rather than following and being situated below the orientational axes of high points in the landscape the Cursus slashes and traverses its way across them until its final termination point on Thickthorn Down. The long barrow in Salisbury Plantation is thus located immediately before an important transition in the relationship of the monument to the local topography. Another important change occurs from this point onwards: the course of the Cursus becomes much less regular and more sinuous, with a number of important changes of direction. From a point roughly 200 m. south of the terminal on Martin Down until just beyond the barrow and the edge of this steep valley the course of the Cursus has a very regular alignment.

Emerging from the valley, the climb to the summit of Bottlebush Down, now traversed by the Cranborne to Sixpenny Handley road, is a steep one. From the summit of Bottlebush Down the impressive barrow traversing the Cursus at right angles, on Gussage Cow Down, becomes visible for the first time, just over 3 km. distant, looking down the Cursus, and the familiar landmark of Penbury Knoll is visible once more looking backwards. The first section of the Cursus ends, as it began, undramatically, dipping away to the south-west down a gentle slope.

Walking at a steady pace, and without stopping, it takes no more than an hour to proceed along the first 4.3 km. stretch of the Cursus. The terrain is gentle and easy until the steep valley just before the end of the first stretch. The second, Gussage, section (Figs. 5.14 and 5.20) is longer, about 5.6 km., and takes about one hour and fifteen minutes to walk. To a much greater extent than the first, it is characterized by long vistas along the Cursus axis as it proceeds down and up two roughly parallel ridges, on both of which long barrows are sited, completely dominating the view. In the first section of the Cursus, after leaving the Martin Down terminal, monuments were absent or hidden. In this second section they were meant to stand out on Gussage Cow Down and Thickthorn Down. Their presence, rather than to be hidden, and to surprise, was to be constantly felt (Fig. 5.21).

The second stretch of the Cursus begins on the midpoint of a slope and runs down to cross the base of a wide and shallow dry valley, the source area of the river Allen. At the point at which the Cursus crosses the valley bottom, where the modern road runs to Wimborne St Giles, the terrain would, in the Neolithic, have been wet and marshy for much of the year. The course of the Cursus crosses over and drops down an ancient Pleistocene river cliff just before reaching the lowest point on the modern road (Fig. 5.22). The banks and ditches of the Cursus were constructed on either side of this topographic feature. One end of it adjoined the northern bank, with the southern bank enclosing the other end with a gap of around 30 m. The drop in relief to anyone walking along the Cursus towards the south-west terminus is both sudden and unexpected. The Cursus here, then, encloses another *surprise* – this time not a hidden monument, but a hidden relict cliff down which the unwary might easily tumble. Until this point the old familiar landmark of Penbury Knoll is visible looking back. Going down the cliff slope it disappears from sight once more at the point at which marshy land is reached, a repetition of the situation encountered in the dry valley towards the end of the first (Pentridge) stretch of the Cursus. Ahead the prominent barrow on Gussage Cow Down dominates the view.

Crossing the modern road the Cursus rises up to the barrow, at first gently and then more steeply. As it does so Penbury Knoll gradually becomes visible once more looking behind. Progressively moving up the slope to approach the long barrow on Gussage Cow Down the barrow outline becomes more and

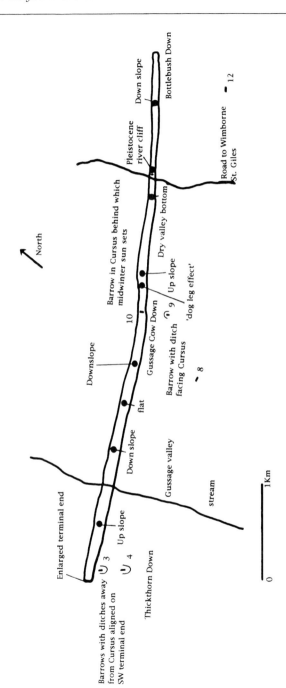

Figure 5.20. Sketch plan of features of the Gussage section of the Cursus (discussed in the text).

Figure 5.21. View along the Gussage section of the Cursus from its beginning on Bottlebush Down up to the northern long barrow on Gussage Cow Down.

Figure 5.22. View back along the Gussage section of the Cursus to Bottlebush Down with the Pleistocene river cliff visible in the centre of the picture with round barrows beyond.

more indistinct, fading away into the skyline. As it does, looking behind, the outline of Penbury Knoll and its accompanying ridges becomes clearer and clearer in the distance. That which is near and in front successively fades away, that which is far away becomes more distinct. The barrow is sited in such a manner that it is completely obscured by the upward slope of the hill until the crest of that hill is almost reached. Altogether it is out of sight for about 550 m. of the course of the Cursus (five minutes' walking time) up the steepest part of the slope. It only looms into sight again at a distance of around 70 m. away.

The ridge of Gussage Cow Down, on which the barrow stands, marks the highest point over which the Cursus crosses from the Bottlebush terminal. The barrow is situated approximately at the midpoint of this second stretch of the monument, and from it the Bottlebush Down terminal and the barrow marking the terminal point on Thickthorn Down would also be visible (it is now concealed by a thick hedge immediately in front of it). As the Cursus climbs up to the Gussage Cow Down barrow it alters direction twice within 230 m., creating what Bradley terms a 'dogleg' effect (Bradley in Barrett *et al.* 1991b: 47). Bradley suggests that this is because the entire Cursus length from the Bottlebush Down terminus was aligned on the Gussage barrow, but that it drifted off course and had to be corrected in the lee of the hill where that barrow could not be observed (ibid.). These changes in the course of the Cursus going up the hill do not make much impression from a map; but they would have had considerable visual impact when viewed from the Bottlebush terminal and *experienced* by those walking up the Cursus. Such a 'dogleg' effect does not occur further on at the point at which the Cursus rises up to adjoin another barrow on Thickthorn Down, where a similar sighting 'problem' occurs, nor is there any evidence for sudden changes in direction where the Cursus crosses the narrow and steep dry valley before climbing up to Bottlebush Down towards the end of the Pentridge section. The 'dogleg' effect may perhaps be more satisfactorily understood by suggesting that it was an intentional design feature put in place to emphasize further the now hidden approach to a monument of central social and symbolic significance.

Gussage Cow Down is a ridge situated midway between the Allen and Gussage valleys. The ridge top itself is orientated NW–SE. The banks of the Cursus do not climb this ridge directly from the bottom of the Allen valley, at right-angles to the direction of the slope, but obliquely, and are set in a roughly diagonal fashion in relation to it. The Cursus thus not only cuts across the natural axis of the landscape as defined by the ridge of Gussage Cow Down with the valleys on either side of it, but it does so obliquely, while also including the 'dogleg' change of direction. Little more contrast with the overall topography, or shape of the land, could be effected than the inclusion of all these three features simultaneously.

By contrast, the two long barrows situated on the ridge top of Gussage Cow Down both duplicate the ridge axes, being orientated SE–NW along their long axes, with their broadest and highest ends facing SE, the norm for Cranborne Chase. These barrows are not sited on the highest point of the ridge top, but a little way below it to the north, at a distance of 240 m. from each other. The long axes of these two barrows are precisely aligned on each other, and, as mentioned above, the northernmost barrow stands in the centre of the Cursus and at right-angles to it. It is this northern barrow that is sited so as to be particularly conspicuous viewed side-on (Figs. 5.7; 5.21 and 5.22). It is intervisible with no less than seven other barrows (see Fig. 5.6), contrasting with the southern barrow, which is only visible from a short distance away, sited as if it were only meant to be seen from the northern barrow and the Cursus. The inference that might be drawn from this is that the southern barrow was intimately related to the northern one, and built with reference to it and its location in the middle of the Cursus.

Penny and Wood (1973: 58–9) and Bradley (in Barrett *et al.* 1991b: 56) have noted and emphasized that the northern barrow on Gussage Cow Down is aligned in such a manner that the midwinter sun can be observed setting behind the barrow on the skyline from the Bottlebush terminal. Dramatically, the rays of the dying sun move from the SE to the NW end of the barrow, with the last flicker of light at the end of the barrow.

Both barrows on Gussage Cow Down are of medium size (50–65 m. long), the southern barrow being a little longer than the northern one. The southern barrow is surrounded by a well-defined U-shaped ditch open towards the northern barrow and the Cursus. The ditches surrounding the northern barrow are now ploughed out, but from aerial photographs (Crawford and Keiller 1923: plate XVI) appear to run parallel to the mound long axis without curving around either end. The barrow is sited off-centre to the Cursus, being much nearer to the NW bank than that to the SE. The reason for this would seem to be fairly obvious – that anyone walking along the Cursus should pass by the side of the barrow rather than walk over it, and do so at the broader and higher SE end, where the mortuary chamber and forecourt area for ritual activities would be sited.

Approaching the northern barrow on Gussage Cow Down the view farther west along the Cursus is completely blocked until the barrow itself is passed (Fig. 5.23). The outline of the southern barrow would be similarly concealed from view by the Cursus banks until the point at which the northern barrow was reached. The Cursus thus contains another surprise: the unexpected barrow to the south, hitherto concealed from view both by virtue of its specific siting and by the Cursus banks. Passing around the southern end of the northern barrow would thus have an added significance, in that this would permit the southern barrow to be seen (Fig. 5.24).

Immediately after passing round the northern barrow the final stretch of the Cursus to Thickthorn Down becomes visible, with the exception of a stretch which runs over the bottom of the Gussage valley and its stream, a tributary of the river Allen (Fig. 5.25). Both the barrows on Thickthorn Down, one located just to the south of the Cursus terminal, and the other aligned on it (see below), would be visible from this point (as mentioned above, they are now concealed by a thick hedge), but not the cross-banks of the Cursus terminal itself, which is located just below the sky-line. The impression given would be that the Cursus itself continued *beyond* this point. From the Bottlebush Down terminal the whole length of the Cursus up to the Gussage North long barrow incorporated within it had been visible. This contrasts interestingly with the situation encountered on reaching that barrow, where the view is visually truncated, concealing the next valley bottom beyond, with the Thickthorn North barrow being located outside the Cursus banks to the left, and the terminus invisible beyond the brow of the hill.

Walking down the slope away from the barrow Penbury Knoll becomes invisible immediately, and the Gussage barrow itself after 300 m. The Cursus descends into a slight dip before rising up again after another 300 m., at which point the barrow behind becomes visible once more. The Cursus then runs over relatively

Figure 5.23. The northern long barrow in the centre of the Cursus on Gussage Cow Down.

Figure 5.24. The southern long barrow on Gussage Cow Down seen from the northern barrow.

Figure 5.25. View south-west from the Gussage North barrow along the final strech of the Cursus up to Thickthorn Down.

flat land for a further 600 m. before finally gently dipping down into the Gussage valley and crossing a stream, which is today water-filled except during dry spells in the summer.

The Cursus then gradually rises up to Thickthorn Down, crossing the slope in a diagonal fashion once more. Half-way up this slope the northern Thickthorn barrow by the Cursus terminal would become invisible on the skyline. The Cursus does not deviate to include the barrow in its course, but runs up the hill and ends just beyond the brow to the north-east of the barrow. The two barrows on Thickthorn Down, in exactly the same manner as the pair on Gussage Cow Down, duplicate the natural axis of the ridge top. They are similarly sited to the north of the highest point of the ridge, and views to the south along the ridge top from them are consequently limited. They are both aligned on the south-east terminal point of the Cursus bank, duplicating the situation encountered at the Martin Down terminal. Both the Thickthorn barrows have U-shaped ditches surrounding the mound, but unlike those at Gussage Cow Down South these ditches are open at the SE rather than the NW end, i.e. away from the Cursus. In other words the relationship of the ditches enclosing the barrows to the south of the Cursus on Gussage Cow Down and on Thickthorn Down is *reversed*.

The Cursus terminal cross-bank and side-bank ends are exceptionally well preserved on Thickthorn Down, and particularly massive (Fig. 5.26). There is no causeway known, so that anyone leaving the Cursus would have to climb out of it over the terminal bank. Bradley has remarked on the massive nature of the Thickthorn terminal cross-bank, suggesting that the Cursus bank here was both considerably higher and larger than those found along the rest of its course and had been deliberately enlarged. He makes the very interesting interpretation that the Cursus cross-bank here had been constructed so as to resemble a massive long barrow (Bradley in Barrett *et al.* 1991b: 51). Building on these observations, it is pertinent to note that the Thickthorn terminal, with its barrow-like cross-bank, is built on sloping ground, with the higher end at the SE and the lower end facing NW, i.e. exactly like the two barrows on Thickthorn Down, with their higher ends at the SE associated with and aligned on it.

What visual impact would this have had on someone approaching the terminal who had not experienced the visual impact of the monument previously, but had progressed along

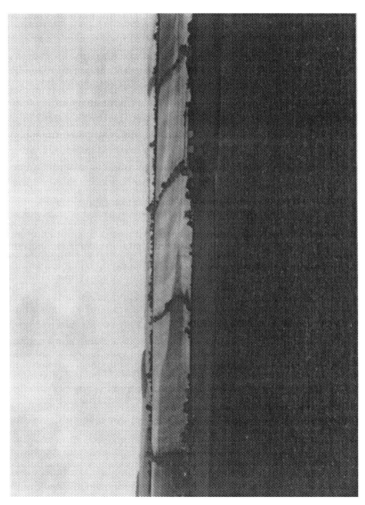

Figure 5.26. The terminal end of the Cursus on Thickthorn Down seen from the end of the Thickthorn North long barrow.

the course of the Cursus from the Martin Down terminus? Going up the slope to Thickthorn Down the two long barrows would be out of sight. Coming to the brow of the hill the Cursus banks would effectively continue to block any view of the Thickthorn barrows; but instead one's vision would be funnelled towards the massively constructed terminal cross-bank blocking any view across the landscape to the west – a feature entirely concealed until this point. On the basis of previous experience of the barrow hidden in the right Cursus bank on the ridge covered by Salisbury Plantation and the barrow placed at right-angles to the Cursus on Gussage Cow Down, together with the orientation and shape of the cross-bank, the obvious (but incorrect) conclusion would be that this was another barrow, but far more massive than anything previously encountered from the Martin Down terminus onwards. The Cursus cross-bank on Thickthorn Down is just over 100 m. long. Emerging from the Cursus, the real long barrows on Thickthorn Down would be visible to the south, and a number of other barrows scattered over the landscape in the distance to the north and west; looking behind to the east, the northern barrow on Gussage Cow Down, and Penbury Knoll, marking the start of the Cursus on Martin Down.

The Empty Place – A Ritual Passage

The precise purpose of the Cursus has remained somewhat enigmatic. Penny and Wood (1973) attempt to explain it as a gigantic astronomical observatory; but most of the solar and lunar alignments they discuss in relation to other long barrows and round barrows in the vicinity seem unconvincing apart from the most basic one, mentioned above – the midwinter sunset behind the Gussage North barrow. Another suggestion common-ly put forward is that the Cursus must be some kind of ceremoni-al or processional way concerned with a cult of the dead (Atkinson 1955: 9). Bradley rightly stresses the manner in which the Cursus links together a series of long barrows, and suggests that there may have been an important distinction between the barrows, possibly related to the rising moon, and the Cursus, with its solar alignment. He argues that:

the entire layout of the Cursus seems to be intended to *exclude* outsiders: only for those inside the great enclosure was the design of the monument apparent. It may be that the building of the Cursus was the ultimate expression of ... changes in attitudes to the dead. It integrated the separate long barrows scattered along the upper limits of the settlement pattern, and at the same time, bound them together in a complex design which could only be appreciated by those who had access to *certain specific points inside the monument*. By incorporating into its structure an important astronomical alignment, those who built it made those developments appear to be part of the functioning of nature (Bradley in Barrett *et al.* 1991b: 58).

Bradley stresses a number of important points in this passage – the ritual function of the Cursus, the fact that it could only be understood from the inside, and an ideological role in naturalizing a set of cultural practices and relating them to the passage of time and the seasons. Rather surprisingly, he also suggests that the Cursus would be unsuitable for processions, as it crosses rivers (ibid.: 47). In the account of walking the Cursus I have repeatedly emphasized the manner in which the spatial structure of the monument and its relationship with topographic features of the landscape and associated barrows constantly surprises someone moving along it for the first time. I want to argue that the experience of walking along it was an essential ingredient in its meaning, and that this movement took place, as described above, from the NE to the SW.

The point about the direction of movement is fairly easily established – the Cursus simply does not make sense when moving down it from the SW end. First, the important solar alignment is not visible from the SW. Second, it might be expected that the monument should end at a dramatic position in the landscape, and the Martin Down terminal, at the top of a gentle slope, does not meet this expectation. Indeed, its location in the landscape more or less repeats that of the earlier Bottlebush terminal, with a long down-slope view. Third, features such as the partially hidden barrow in the bank of the Pentridge section of the Cursus, the hidden Pleistocene river cliff, and the massively enlarged Cursus terminal cross-bank on Thickthorn Down in the Gussage section would have little or no visual or somatic impact when approached from the NW, and would not surprise.

The Cursus is a massive linear space bounded by banks with external ditches curving round at its ends, with the highest and most massive terminal cross-banks in the SW. In its linearity, external ditches and emphasized terminal point it resembles a massive unfilled long barrow. It differs from most barrows in its overall orientation and relationship with the landscape, crossing rather than following its contours, for much of its length. The Cursus was deliberately designed so as to include two previously constructed barrows within it, and the orientations of others at both terminals are clearly related to it. In this sense it presenced the past in the present, and part of its meaning was constituted by its relationship to the barrows and the specific manner in which it connected them together.

The Gussage Cursus has a clear symmetry in its arrangement. It runs down a slope, over an ancient river cliff, crosses water, moves up a slope to the ridge top where the Gussage Cow Down barrow is located, moves down another slope, crosses water and runs up to its terminus on Thickthorn Down. It is not hard to imagine how such a monument worked in terms of initiation ceremonies involving liminal states and rituals of reversal. Novices are taken out of the mundane everyday world and into the enclosed and bounded space of the Cursus. They move along, going down-slope, shut out from the world in the direction of the dying sun, stumble down the concealed ancient river cliff, and then cross wet land to reach the Gussage barrow in the centre of the Cursus. They experience it moving out of sight and changes in the Cursus direction. When they eventually approach the bar-row they move round its higher SE end with great ceremonial, and see for the first time the barrow outside the Cursus to the south, with its open unenclosed lower end facing them, and are instructed with tales of the ancestors and supernatural beings. Ahead on Thickthorn Down two other barrows are visible, but outside the Cursus. They move down the slope, cross water and continue up-slope to Thickthorn Down, where the barrows are concealed and the massive barrow-like terminus blocks the view. Climbing out of the Cursus they return to the everyday world with the ditches around the Thickthorn barrows in the 'right' place at the lower end.

There are an obvious set of structural contrasts here: between high and low, down-slope and up-slope, wet and dry, barrows with ditches open at the NW and then the SE ends, barrows within the monument and barrows outside it, and plays on the visibility and invisibility of barrows in relation to movement, creating a series of contrasts and surprises. Within the enclosed world of the Cursus the Gussage Cow Down barrow is itself placed at a high, dry point within liminal space, and water must be crossed to reach and to leave it.

The Pentridge extension to the Cursus modifies the simpler pattern of the initial Gussage Cursus to introduce more contrasts and surprises. The extended Cursus from Martin Down to Thickthorn Down begins, like the Gussage Cursus, down-slope; it ends up-slope. It begins just to the north of the most dominant and familiar landmark in the area, Penbury Knoll, visible from virtually all the long barrows in the Cranborne Chase group. It now both begins and ends with barrows located outside the Cursus, aligned on the SE terminal point. In approximately the mid-point of each stretch barrows are included within the monument at high points; but their relationship to the Cursus itself is reversed, at first respecting and then cross-cutting its axis. The first barrow inside the Cursus is hidden, the second highly visible. The first barrow stands on its own, the second is associated with a barrow outside the Cursus. Both barrows on Thickthorn Down are outside the Cursus. So in relationship to the long barrows with which it is associated the extended Cursus from its starting-point has varying degrees of incorporation – total in the Pentridge section (the barrow forms part of the Cursus banks), partial on Gussage Cow Down (one barrow is outside the Cursus). The Pentridge section of Cursus at first parallels high ground to its left; and then, once the first barrow is reached, this relationship is reversed, and it crosses rather than follows valleys. The pattern is one of symmetries and differences, repetitions and reversals, requiring, as Bradley rightly stresses, an insider's knowledge and detailed ritual instruction to understand them and their significance. The Cursus, through its form and the connections it creates with other monuments, establishes through formalized successional movement along it, a spatial story.

The Cursus represents a formalized structuring of the experience of landscape by those entering and using it. It acted not only as a conduit of movement, but as a barrier blocking a less structured encounter with the barrows on Cranborne Chase. As Barrett (1994) has recently argued with reference to the somewhat later ceremonial monuments of Durrington Walls, Avebury and Stonehenge, it is highly unlikely that it was formally planned and conceived. It represents rather a series of construction projects that were modified and whose meaning and significance became altered though time, thus transforming the biographies, myths and encounters of people with the landscape. The very act of people coming together to construct the monument, camping nearby for several weeks or months, to re-establish, augment and develop it, was important in itself and not simply a matter of the creation of a container for various forms of subsequent activity.

It is not unlikely that, on Cranborne Chase, part of the narrative meanings of the Dorset Cursus were linked not only to initiation rites, but also to the themes of death and the regeneration of life. It may have operated as a linear conduit through which both bodies and bones were being moved between the barrows in the central part of the Chase and Hambledon Hill. Bodies were perhaps being taken out of Cranborne Chase to a death island of the setting sun immediately beyond its margins to the west, and being allowed to decompose, with selected bones being returned to the barrows in the central ritual arena of the Chase itself. The pollution of death was thus being removed and dry, clean and ritually pure bones returned. Given the massive effort required to construct the Cursus, the barrows themselves, and the enclosures on Hambledon Hill, and the long-distance movement of pottery, axes and other materials during the Neolithic, such a system of corpse movement does not appear inherently unlikely. On Hambledon Hill artefacts were carefully offered and deposited in the pits inside the enclosure and in the ditches as if they were bones. In turn the bones of the skeleton became treated as artefacts, being deposited in the barrows and circulating among the living.

Conclusion

The slight early Neolithic 'settlement' evidence, contemporary with the construction of the barrows, the Cursus and Hambledon Hill, suggests that Cranborne Chase may have been an area that was not permanently settled, but periodically visited by a number of surrounding social groups, to perform rituals, bury the dead and manipulate ancestral bones. The escarpment peripheries were marked out by barrows aligned along its axes, emphasizing transition up to an important sacred space. The barrows situated in the centre of the Chase were situated so as to duplicate the contours of the land, while the Cursus dramatically cuts across them, linking the monuments together. Hambledon Hill was a heavily ritualized death island to the west, to which bodies were taken in processions and from which ancestral bones were circulated back to the barrows on the Chase. In this area the visual relationship between monuments and their sequential ordering along the formalized path of movement marked out by the Cursus was as essential a part of their meaning as the ritual topography itself that these monuments helped to create and sustain.

Chapter 6

Conclusion: Ideology and Place: Restructuring the Connections

'The flow of movement is a flow of the mind.' I have argued that during the Mesolithic, in all three study areas, ancestral connections between living populations and the past were embodied in the Being of the landscape and an emotional attachment to place that had a generalized power and significance in relation to human activity as a series of known, named and significant places linked by paths of movement to which populations repeatedly returned during their seasonal activity rounds. These Mesolithic populations made relatively little impact on the land apart from establishing clearings around their camp-sites and burning off areas of woodland to stimulate browse.

In the earlier Neolithic the relationship between populations and the landscape became restructured and took on a different form. The ancestral powers and meanings in the landscape now became actively *appropriated* by individuals and groups through the construction and use of chambered tombs, long cairns and long barrows, and on Cranborne Chase by the Cursus and the enclosures on Hambledon Hill. These monuments served to make permanent, anchor, fix and visually draw out for perception the connections between people and the land for the first time. Ancestral powers now became double. The tombs presenced and marked out the bones of the ancestral dead in the landscape. In so doing they visibly brought the presence of the ancestral past to consciousness. Their specific morphological characteristics and their landscape settings also served to relate the bones of previous generations to a more generalized ancestral power embodied in the topography and symbolic geography of place and paths of movement which had already been constituted in the Mesolithic. The location of important points in the external world became captured in the orientation of morphological features of the monuments and their placement in the landscape. Their settings were deliberately chosen to fix a certain vantage point in relation to perception of the world beyond. During the Mesolithic the significance of place was understood in terms of its setting in the landscape. In the Neolithic this was reversed – the landscape was now understood in terms of its relationship to the setting of the monuments.

In other words, the setting of place became much more anchored. Megalith building and long barrow construction implies a need to represent in a physical form and capture permanently ancestral connections with the landscape. In southwest Wales this was effected by constructing monuments near to important topographical markers in the land such as rock outcrops. In the Black Mountains the long axis of the chambered cairn was of paramount significance. It imposed a form, a directional line across the topography, producing an axis directing vision in a prescribed direction outward from the monument itself and pointing towards escarpment spurs or along prescribed routes of movements along the Usk and Wye valleys. On Cranborne Chase, the long barrows, rather than directing vision beyond themselves, outward towards topographic features, are sedimented into the lie of the land itself, following its contours.

Discussing the three different landscapes, and moving from west to east across Wales and southern England, I have attempted to take the reader on a textual journey involving a number of basic transformations. First we move from a case of a lack of monument visibility to intervisibility. Second, there is an increasing emphasis on movement; and third, there is a greater emphasis on the elimination of difference in monument form from case 1 to case 3. Finally there is also a basic contrast between Cranborne Chase and the situation in south-west Wales and the Black Mountains. The relationship between monuments of fundamentally different forms and uses (the barrows, the Cursus and the causewayed enclosure on Hambledon Hill) was as important here as was the relationship to the topography. Siting a barrow on Cranborne Chase was much more intimately linked to the position of other previously constructed barrows than it appears to have been in Wales. Increasingly, through the construction of the Cursus, formalizing one path of movement between the barrows, and, no doubt, blocking others, one type of monument could only be 'read' and understood here in relation to the others.

The building of the monuments prevented the ritual and mythological significance of particular places being lost and forgotten. They stabilized both cultural memory of place and connections between places. The cultural appropriation in the Neolithic of already established ancestral powers in the landscape through monument building served to increase its symbolic potency and power. Through the mediation of the tomb time became frozen, with the drawing of the past into the present. The tomb *objectified* ancestral powers in the landscape. In this way these powers became not just subjects of knowledge but objects of knowledge too, resources to be worked upon and manipulated for the sectional social interests of individuals or particular social groups.

The architectural forms of cairn and barrow, Cursus and causewayed enclosure, in their different ways, signify a will to make ancestral powers in the land *visible*, to be seen and remembered, but always from a particular perspective provided by the vantage points of the monuments. As we move around in space our perspective of the landscape alters. What the monuments did, in their different ways, was to freeze perspective through the architectural lens of the monuments themselves – their orientations, entrances and exits, façades, forecourts and passage-ways. They are then about establishing *control* over topographic perspective and the individual's possibilities for interpreting the world. Experience of the landscape in the Neolithic became mediated and channelled through fixed and permanent architectural form. Landscape perception, now being structured through monuments and relationships between them, became far more 'focused'. Experience of the ancestral past now came into being within the specific setting of monuments and their relationships to the outside world. This, in turn, is linked with control of knowledges of the ancestral past which are mediated through the cultural form of the monument and the character of the deposits left in and around it. Ancestral powers in the landscape could now only be deciphered from experiencing them at the site of the tomb or by passing down the Cursus or entering a causewayed enclosure. This in effect represents a closing down and restriction of a variety of 'points of view' – both literal and metaphorical. The monuments both deployed and captured an ancestral history. Acting as mnemonic markers they coded historicity and sacred power in particular places, creating a hierarchy of valued points in the landscape on pathways channelling movement through it and sustaining knowledge of it. This logic, involving a re-ordering of the visible, constituted a vital component of power relations during the Neolithic, serving to differentiate between those who were included in the knowledges required to decipher the landscape and those who were excluded.

In this respect it seems pertinent to note that, considering the overall distribution of megalithic monuments in Wales and southern England, where we find chambered tombs or long barrows we also usually have evidence of a substantial amount of Mesolithic activity. In areas where there are no monuments there is little or no Mesolithic evidence either. Such a generalization could also be extended to other areas of Europe, such as Brittany, the Netherlands and much of southern Scandinavia.

'Our body, to the extent that it moves itself about, that is, to the extent that it is inseparable from a view of the world and is that view itself brought into existence, is the condition of possibility ... of all expressive operations and all acquired views which constitute the cultural world' (Merleau-Ponty 1962: 388). At one level monument construction solved the existential problem of how to experience the natural world and the powers embedded in it when none of the perspective views of it as the human body moves through space can exhaust it. Horizons for experience are always open and changing. Through the culturally embedded horizon of the tomb and its setting the landscape became visibly encultured. In turn, the relation of the tomb to the landscape served to naturalize the ancestral powers embodied in the cultural form of the monument and its bone and artefact deposits. They are being represented as part of an immutable natural order of things. The natural world as mediated through the tomb becomes the horizon of all horizons, the style of all possible styles, guaranteeing for experience a *given* rather than a *willed* unity as a framework for knowledge of the social and its connection with the past. The monument draws together and serves to coalesce the natural and the cultural as a framework for experiencing and understanding the world. What appears – the monument – 'hides' contexts in which it does not appear. It captures and draws attention, domesticating the view of the landscape. The monuments, then, are to do with the formation and stabilization of attitudes toward the world. They acted as signifiers of part of a structure of knowledge, an iconography of human intentions, a resource for power and social control. With the advent of monument construction the landscape increasingly starts to become not just a subject of human symbolic labour but an object of that labour too.

In the above paragraph I wrote of the view of the landscape in the Neolithic's, becoming 'domesticated', and I now want briefly to explore how this might relate to subsistence practices. It appears that, in the areas I have considered, cultivation was probably not important; but the herding of domesticates, particularly cattle, began to assume an increasing significance during the Neolithic. The herding and tending of animals formed part and parcel of the new 'order of thought', manifested so dramatically through monument construction and use. Domestic animals during the Neolithic had a much greater symbolic exchange-value than their utilitarian use-value as food on the hoof. Part of the process of thinking about the landscape in a fresh way now involved *thinking it through animals*. There are two main aspects to this. First, as I have argued at length elsewhere (Tilley in press), the symbolic potential and evaluation of food derived from domesticates, as opposed to that acquired through foraging, constituted a major preoccupation in exchange, feasting and ritual. It is not surprising, then, that the vast bulk of domestic animal bones known from the British Neolithic occur on ceremonial rather than domestic sites, and that many of these deposits are highly structured, i.e. come from specific parts of the animal, such as the preponderance of skulls and mandibles found in the Cursus ditches, discussed above. Meat from domestic animals was exotic and highly prestigious, and became a requirement for ritual practice – quite literally food for thought. Although still probably contributing the bulk of the subsistence base, food acquired from foraging gradually became down-graded in status during the course of the Neolithic, and producing food for ritual events provided a major stimulant for an increasing emphasis on domesticates.

Second, in general terms, it might be expected that there would be more ideological continuity in terms of the importance attached to paths, as opposed to boundaries, between hunter–gatherer–fishers and populations which had incorporated a pastoral component, than between hunters and settled agricultural societies. Herding meant changing attitudes to grazing land, to property and inheritance, to over-wintering stock, food, ritual and ceremonial. Herding involved seasonal movements along pathways through the landscape, as in the Mesolithic, but with altogether different connotations. It obviously required a great deal more social commitment and ideological investment in the process of this movement, which would, as did the monuments, increasingly serve to inscribe and 'fix' the landscape. Moving animals along paths already in use from the Mesolithic *objectified* them in just the same way as I have argued that monuments 'captured' the ancestral connotations of topographic features of the landscape. The movements of animals would physically inscribe these paths across the landscape much more prominently than the feet of hunter–gatherers following the movements of game, and it would become increasingly difficult (both in practical and symbolic terms) to take different ways. The monuments, then, sedimented the symbolic potency of locales in the landscape, domestic animals the paths of movement between them and the ceremonies conducted in and around them. This is not to impy any economic determinancy. It is rather a matter of a social, political and ideological transformation that had profound consequences for an entire Neolithic way of life, involving both continuity and change from the Mesolithic.

I have suggested that, as cultural markers, one of the purposes of the megaliths in the Black Mountains and south-west Wales and the long barrows on Cranborne Chase would seem to have been to draw attention to the symbolic and social significance of the natural topography and markers within it, such as the coast, rivers, rock outcrops, spurs, escarpments and ridges. Such markers and places were almost certainly in use during the Mesolithic preceding the construction of these Neolithic monuments. The Mesolithic hunter–gatherers would have used them, as they can be used today, as reference points and orientational foci. These were obvious locations for stopping, resting, telling stories, observing game movements. As such they would be named and be invested with narratives and mythologies. In a sense the rock outcrops, cliffs and escarpment edges of South-West Wales and the Black Mountains are natural untamed non-domesticated 'megaliths' or stone groups.

The occurence of flint scatters at these locales would have had considerable significance during the Mesolithic and early Neolithic for a recognition, reading and understanding of place. Like the difference between primary forest and regenerating areas, differences in the composition of these scatters- waste, flakes, cores, microlith forms and discarded tools would act so as to recall memories of previous visits, activities, events and seasons. Reading these signs from places visited by previous generations Mesolithic archaeologists would also be able to infer, like the contemporary archaeologist, the types of activities that had taken place.

What happens in the Neolithic is the constitution of a different sense of time, place and social identity, through monument building, and also by means of the herding of domesticates on pathways across the land. Cultural markers are being used to create a new sense of place, harnessed to legitimize patterns of social control relating to restricting access to knowledges deemed essential to group reproduction, while continuing to make reference or lay claim to already established ancestral connections with, and pathways through, the landscape. An already encultured landscape becomes refashioned, its meanings now controlled by the imposition of the cultural form of the constructed monument.

References

ApSimon, A. (1976), 'A view of the early prehistory of Wales', in G. Boon and J. Lewis (eds), *Welsh Antiquity*, Cardiff: University of Wales Press

Arnold, J., Green, M., Lewis, B. and Bradley, R. (1988), 'The Mesolithic of Cranborne Chase', *Proceedings of the Dorset Natural History and Archaeological Society*, 110: 117–25

Ashbee, P. (1984), *The Earthen Long Barrow in Britain*, Norwich: Geo Books

Atkinson, R. (1955), 'The Dorset Cursus', *Antiquity*, 29: 4–9

Barker, C. T. (1992), *The Chambered Tombs of South-West Wales*, Oxbow Monograph 14, Oxford: Oxbow Books

Barrett, J. (1994), *Fragments from Antiquity*, Oxford: Blackwell.

Barrett, J. and Bradley, R. (1991), 'The Cranborne Chase project and its publication', in J. Barrett, R. Bradley and M. Hall (eds)

Barrett, J., Bradley, R. and Hall, M. (eds), (1991a), *Papers on the Prehistoric Archaeology of Cranborne Chase*, Oxbow Monograph 11, Oxford: Oxbow Books

Barrett, J., Bradley, R. and Green, M. (1991b), *Landscape, Monuments and Society. The Prehistory of Cranborne Chase*, Cambridge: Cambridge University Press

Barth, F. (1975), *Ritual and Knowledge among the Baktaman*, New Haven: Yale University Press

Basso, K. (1984), '"Stalking with stories": names, places and moral narratives among the western Apache', in E. Bruner (ed.) *Text, Play and Story*, Prospect Heights, Illinois: Waveland Press

Bender, B. (1992), 'Theorising landscapes, and the prehistoric landscapes of Stonehenge', *Man*, 27: 735–55

Bender, B. (ed.) (1993), *Landscape: Politics and Perspectives*, Oxford: Berg

Berndt, R. (1972), 'The Walmadjeri and Gugadja', in M. Bicchieri (ed.), *Hunters and Gatherers Today*, New York: Holt, Rinehart and Winston

Berndt, R. (1974), *Australian Aboriginal Religion*, Leiden: E. J. Brill

Berndt, R. (1976), 'Territoriality and the problem of demarcating sociocultural space', in N. Peterson (ed.), *Tribes and Boundaries in Australia*, New Jersey: Humanities Press

Berndt, R. and Berndt, C. (eds) (1965), *Aboriginal Man in Australia*, London: Angus and Robertson

Berridge, P. (1980), 'Waun Fingen Felin', *Archaeology in Wales* 20: 19–20

Binford, L. (1978), *Nunamiut Ethnoarchaeology*, London: Academic Press

Binford, L. (1980), '"Willow smoke and dog's tails": hunter–gatherer settlement systems and archaeological site formation', *American Antiquity*, 45: 4–20

Bradley, R. (1984), *The Social Foundations of Prehistoric Britain*, London: Longman

Bradley, R. and Gardiner, J. (eds), (1984), *Neolithic Studies. A Review of Some Current Research*, Oxford: British Archaeological Reports 133

Bradley, R., Cleal, R., Gardiner, J., Green, M. and Bowden, M. (1984), 'The Neolithic sequence in Cranborne Chase', in R. Bradley and J. Gardiner (eds)

Britnell, W. (1984), 'Gwernvale: discussion', in W. Britnell and H. Savory

Britnell, W. (1991), 'Penywyrlod, Talgarth', *Archaeology in Wales*, 31: 14

Britnell, W. and Savory, H. (1984), *Gwernvale and Penywyrlod: Two Neolithic Long Cairns in the Black Mountains of Brecknock*, Cardiff: Cambrian Archaeological Monographs No. 2

Brody, H. (1981), *Maps and Dreams*, Vancouver: Douglas and McIntyre

Burke, T. (1966), 'Excavations at Pant Sychbant, Penderyn (Breckn.)', *Bulletin of the Board of Celtic Studies*, 22: 78–87

Buttimer, A. and Seamon, D. (eds) (1980), *The Human Experience of Space and Place*, London: Croom Helm

Cantrill, T. (1915), 'Flint chipping floors in south west Pembrokeshire', *Archaeologia Cambrensis*, Sixth Series, 15: 157–210

Care, V. (1979), 'The production and distribution of Mesolithic axes in southern England', *Proceedings of the Prehistoric Society*, 45: 93–102

Caseldine, A. (1990), *Environmental Archaeology in Wales*, Lampeter: St David's University College

Catt, J., Green, M. and Arnold, J. (1980), 'Naleds in a Wessex downland valley', *Proceedings of the Dorset Natural History and Archaeology Society*, 102: 69–75

Chase, A. (1984), 'Belonging to country, territory, identity and environment in Cape York peninsula, Northern Australia', *Oceania Monograph*, 27: 104–22

Chorley, R. and Haggett, P. (eds) (1967), *Models in Geography*, London: Methuen

Clark, J. (1936), 'Report on flint objects', Appendix in C. Drew and S. Piggott (1936)

Clarke, D. (ed.), (1972), *Models in Archaeology*, London: Methuen

Clarke, D. (ed.), (1977), *Spatial Archaeology*, London: Academic Press

Cloutman, E. (1983), Studies of the Vegetational History of the Black Mountain Range, South Wales, Unpublished Ph.D. thesis, University of Wales

Corcoran, C. (1969), 'The Cotswold-Severn Group', in T. Powell, C. Corcoran, F. Lynch, and J. Scott, *Megalithic Enquiries in the West of Britain*, Liverpool: Liverpool University Press.

Cosgrove, D. (1984), *Social Formation and Symbolic Landscape*, London: Croom Helm

Cosgrove, D. (1989), 'Geography is everywhere: culture and symbolism in human landscapes', in D. Gregory and R. Walford (eds), *Horizons in Human Geography*, London: Macmillan

Cosgrove, D. and Daniels, S. (1988), 'Introduction: iconography and landscape', in D. Cosgrove and S. Daniels (eds), *The Iconography of Landscape*, Cambridge: Cambridge University Press

Crampton, C. and Webley, D. (1966), 'A section through the Mynydd Troed long barrow, Brecknock', *Bulletin of the Board of Celtic Studies*, 22: 71–7

Crawford, O. and Keiller, A. (1923), *Wessex from the Air*, Oxford: Oxford University Press

Daniels, S. (1989), 'Marxism, culture and the duplicity of landscape' in Peet and Thrift (eds)

David, A. (1990), 'Some aspects of the human presence in west Wales during the Mesolithic', in C. Bonsall (ed.), *The Mesolithic in Europe*, Edinburgh: John Donald

de Certeau, M. (1984), *The Practice of Everyday Life*, Berkeley: University of California Press

Dixon, R. (1976), 'Tribes, languages and other boundaries in northeast Queensland', in N. Peterson (ed.) *Tribes and Boundaries in Australia*, New Jersey: Humanities Press

Drew, C. and Piggott, S. (1936), 'Excavation of long barrow 163a on Thickthorn Down, Dorset', *Proceedings of the Prehistoric Society*, 2: 77–96.

Duncan, S. (1989), 'What is locality?', in Peet and Thrift (eds)

Edmonds, M. (1993), 'Interpreting causewayed enclosures in the past and the present', in C. Tilley (ed.)

Entwistle, R. and Bowden, M. (1991), 'Cranborne Chase: the molluscan evidence', in J. Barrett, R. Bradley and M. Hall (eds)

Evans, A. and Jones, M. (1979), ' The plant remains', Appendix in G. Wainwright, *Gussage All Saints: An Iron Age settlement in Dorset*, London: HMSO

Farrar, R. (1951), 'Archaeological fieldwork in Dorset in 1951: a Neolithic causewayed enclosure at Hambledon Hill', *Proceedings of the Dorset Natural History and Archaeology Society*, 73: 105–6

Fisher, P. (1991), 'The physical environment of Cranborne Chase', in J. Barrett, R. Bradley and M. Hall (eds)

Foucault, M. (1977), *Discipline and Punish*, New York: Vintage

Foucault, M. (1986), 'Of other spaces', *Diacritics*, 16: 22–7

Gamble, C. (1986), 'Hunter–gatherers and the origin of states', in J. Hall (ed.), *States in History*, Oxford: Blackwell.

Gardiner, J. (1984), 'Lithic distributions and Neolithic settlement patterns in central southern England', in R. Bradley and J. Gardiner (eds)

Giddens, A. (1979), *Central Problems in Social Theory*, London: Macmillan

Giddens, A. (1981), *A Contemporary Critique of Historical Materialism*, London: Macmillan

Giddens, A. (1984), *The Constitution of Society*, Cambridge: Polity Press

Gold, J. and Burgess, J. (eds), (1982), *Valued Environments*, London: Allen and Unwin

Gordon-Williams, J. (1926), 'The Nab Head chipping floor', *Archaeologia Cambrensis*, 81: 86–111.

Goudie, A. (1987), 'Geography and archaeology: the growth of a relationship', in J. Wagstaff (ed.)

Gregory, D. (1978), *Ideology, Science and Human Geography*, London: Hutchinson

Gregory, D. and Urry, J. (eds), (1985), *Social Relations and Spatial Structures*, London: Macmillan

Grimes, W. (1932), 'Surface flint industries around Solva, Pembrokeshire', *Archaeologia Cambrensis*, 86: 179–220.

Grimes, W. (1936a), 'The megalithic monuments of Wales', *Proceedings of the Prehistoric Society*, 2: 106–39.

Grimes, W. (1936b), 'The long cairns of the Brecknockshire Black Mountains', *Archaeologia Cambrensis*, 259–82.

Grimes, W. (1939a), 'Bedd yr Afanc', *Proceedings of the Prehistoric Society*, 5: 258

Grimes, W. (1939b), 'The excavation of the Ty-Isaf long cairn, Brecknockshire', *Proceedings of the Prehistoric Society*, 5: 119–42

Grimes, W. (1948), 'Pentre Ifan burial chamber, Pembrokeshire', *Archaeologia Cambrensis*, 100: 3–23

Grinsell, L. (1938–40), 'Hampshire barrows', *Proceedings of the Hampshire Field Club*, Vol XIV: 9–40; 195–365

Grinsell, L. (1957), 'Archaeological gazetteer', *Victoria County History Wiltshire* 1,1, London.

Grinsell, L. (1959), *Dorset Barrows*, Dorchester: Longman

Guidieri, R. and Pellizzi, F. (1981), 'Shadows. Nineteen tableaux on the cult of the dead in Malekula, eastern Melanesia', *Res*, 2: 6–71.

Hallowell, A. (1955), *Culture and Experience*, Philadelphia: University of Pennsylvania Press

Harrington, J. (1916), *The Ethnogeography of the Tewa Indians*, Washington DC: Annual Report of the Bureau of American Ethnology 29

Harrison, S. (1988), 'Magical exchange of the preconditions of production in a Sepik river village', *Man*, 23: 319–33

Harvey, D. (1969), *Explanation in Geography*, London: Arnold

Harvey, D. (1973), *Social Justice and the City*, London: Arnold

Heidegger, M. (1972), 'Building dwelling thinking' in M. Heidegger, *Basic Writings*, (ed. D. Krell), London: Routledge

Higgs, E. (1959), 'Excavations at a Mesolithic site at Downton, near Salisbury, Wiltshire', *Proccedings of the Prehistoric Society*, 25: 209–32

Hirsch, P. and O'Hanlon, M. (eds) (in press) *The Anthropology of Landscape: Between Place and Space*, Oxford: Oxford University Press

Hodder, I. (1982a), *Symbols in Action*, Cambridge: Cambridge University Press

Hodder, I. (ed.), (1982b), *Symbolic and Structural Archaeology*, Cambridge: Cambridge University Press

Hodder, I. (1986), *Reading the Past*, Cambridge: Cambridge University Press

Hodder, I. (1987), 'Converging traditions: the search for symbolic meanings in archaeology and geography', in J. Wagstaff (ed.)

Hodder, I. (1992), *Theory and Practice in Archaeology*, London: Routledge

Hodder, I. and Orton, C. (1976), *Spatial Analysis in Archaeology*, Cambridge: Cambridge University Press

Hugh-Jones, C. (1979), *From the Milk River: Spatial and Temporal Processes in Northwest Amazonia*, Cambridge: Cambridge University Press

Ingold, T. (1986), *The Appropriation of Nature*, Manchester: Manchester University Press

Ingold, T. (1992), 'Culture and the perception of the environment', in E. Croll and D. Parkin (eds), *Bush Base: Forest Farm*, London: Routledge

Ingold, T. (1993), 'The temporality of landscape', *World Archaeology*, 25 (2): 152–74

Jackson, J. (1936), 'Report on the animal remains', Appendix in Drew and Piggott

Jacobi, R. (1980), 'The early Holocene settlement of Wales', in J. Taylor (ed.), *Culture and Environment in Prehistoric Wales*, Oxford: British Archaeological Reports 76

Jacobi, R. (1981), 'The last hunters in Hampshire', in S. Shennan and R. Schadla Hall (eds), *The Archaeology of Hampshire*, Aldershot: Hampshire Field Club and Archaeology Society

Jarman, M., Bailey, G. and Jarman, H. (eds) (1982), *Early European Agriculture*, Cambridge: Cambridge University Press

Jones, R. (1990), 'Hunters of the Dreaming: some ideational, economic and ecological parameters of the Australian Aboriginal productive system', in D. Yen and J. Mummery (eds), *Pacific Production Systems: Approaches to Economic Prehistory*, Canberra: Australian National University

Kahn, M. (1990), 'Stone-faced ancestors: the spatial anchoring of myth in Wamira, Papua New Guinea', *Ethnology*, 29: 51–66

Kinnes, I. (1988), 'The cattleship potemkin: reflections on the first neolithic in Britain', in J. Barrett and I. Kinnes (eds), *The Archaeology of Context*, Sheffield: University of Sheffield

Kinnes, I. (1992), *Non-Megalithic Long Barrows and Allied Structures in the British Neolithic*, London: British Museum Occasional Paper 52

Kirk, T. (1993), 'Space, subjectivity, power and hegemony: megaliths and long mounds in earlier Neolithic Brittany', in C. Tilley (ed.), *Interpretative Archaeology*, Oxford: Berg

Küchler, S. (1993), 'Landscape as memory: the mapping of process and its representation in a Melanesian society', in B. Bender (ed.),

Lacaille, A. and Grimes, W. (1955), 'The prehistory of Caldey', *Archaeologia Cambrensis*, 104: 85–165

Layton, R. (n.d.), 'Relating to country in the Western desert', unpublished manuscript. To appear in P. Hirsch and M. O'Hanlon (eds)

Leach, A. (1913), 'Stone implements from soil drifts, south Pembroke', *Archaeologia Cambrensis*, Sixth Series, 13: 391–433

Leach, A. (1918), 'Flint-working sites on the submerged land (Submerged Forest) bordering the Pembrokeshire coast', *Proceedings of the Geological Association*, 29 (2): 46–67

Leach, A. (1933), 'Stone implements from the Nab Head, St. Bride's Pembrokeshire', *Archaeologia Cambrensis*, 87: 229–36

Legge, A. (1991), 'The animal remains from six sites at Down Farm, Woodcutts', in J. Barrett, R. Bradley and M. Hall (eds)

Leenhardt, M. (1930), 'Notes d'ethnologie Néo-Calédonienne', Paris: *Travaux et Mémoires de l'Institut d'Ethnologie*, Vol. 8

Lewis, B. and Coleman, R. (1984), 'Pentridge Hill, Dorset: trial excavations', *Procceedings of the Dorset Natural History and Archaeology Society*, 104: 59–65

Lewis, M. (1990), The Prehistory of Coastal S. W. Wales 7500–3600 BP. An Interdisciplinary Palaeoenvironmental and Archaeological Investigation, University of Wales: Unpublished Ph.D. dissertation

Luff, R., Brothwell, D. and O'Connor, T. (1984), 'The human and animal remains', Appendix in Britnell and Savory

Lynch, F. (1972), 'Portal dolmens in the Nevern valley, Pembrokeshire', in F. Lynch and C. Burgess (eds), *Prehistoric Man in Wales and the West*, Bath: Adams and Dart

Lynch, F. (1975), 'Excavations at Carreg Samson megalithic tomb, Mathry, Pembrokeshire', *Archaeologia Cambrensis*, 124: 15–35

Lynch, F. (1976), 'Towards a chronology of megalithic tombs in Wales' in G. Boon and J. Lewis (eds), *Welsh Antiquity: essays presented to H. N. Savory*, Cardiff: National Museum of Wales

Malinowski, B. (1922), *Argonauts of the Western Pacific*, London: Routledge Kegan Paul

Mellars, P. (1976), 'Fire, ecology, animal populations and man: a study of some ecological relationships in prehistory', *Proceedings of the Prehistoric Society*, 42: 15–45

Mercer, R. (1980), *Hambledon Hill: A Neolithic Landscape*, Edinburgh: Edinburgh University Press

Mercer, R. (1981), 'Excavations at Carn Brea, Illogan, Cornwall', *Cornish Archaeology*, 20: 1–204.

Mercer, R. (1988), 'Hambledon Hill, Dorset, England', in C. Burgess, P. Topping, C. Mordant and H. Maddison (eds), *Enclosures and Defences in the Neolithic of Western Europe*, Oxford: British Archaeological Reports 403

Merleau-Ponty, M. (1962), *Phenomenology of Perception*, London: Routledge

Miller, D. and Tilley, C. (eds) (1984), *Ideology, Power and Prehistory*, Cambridge: Cambridge University Press

Momaday, S. (1974), ' Native American attitudes to the environment', in W. Capps (ed.), *Seeing With a Native Eye: Essays on Native American Religion*, New York: Harper Forum Books

Morphy, H. (1989), 'From dull to brilliant: the aesthetics of spiritual power among the Yolungu', *Man*, 34 (1): 21–40

Morphy, H. (1991), *Ancestral Connections*, Chicago: Chicago University Press

Morphy, H. (n.d.), 'Landscape: the reproduction of the ancestral past', unpublished manuscript. To appear in P. Hirsch and M. O'Hanlon (eds)

Mountford, C. (1965), *Ayers Rock. Its People, Their Beliefs and Their Art*, Honolulu: East–West Center Press

Munn, N. (1970), 'The transformation of subjects into objects in Walbiri and Pitjantjatjara myth' in R. Berndt (ed.), *Australian Aboriginal Anthropology*, Nedlands: University of Western Australia Press

Munn, N. (1973), 'The spatial presentation of cosmic order in Walbiri iconography', in A. Forge (ed.), *Primitive Art and Society*, Oxford: Oxford University Press

Munn, N. (1986), *Walbiri Iconography*, Chicago: University of Chicago Press

Nelson, R. (1983), *Make Prayers to the Raven*, Chicago: University of Chicago Press

Ortiz, A. (1969), *The Tewa World*, Chicago: University of Chicago Press

Parmentier, R. (1987), *The Sacred Remains*, Chicago: University of Chicago Press

Parsons, E. (1939), *Pueblo Indian Religion*, 2 Vols, Chicago: Chicago University Press

Peet, R. and Thrift, N. (eds) (1989), *New Models in Geography*, Vol. 2, London: Unwin Hyman

Penning-Rosewell, E. and Lowenthal, D. (eds) (1986), *Landscape Meanings and Values*, London: Allen and Unwin

Penny, A. and Wood, J. (1973), 'The Dorset cursus complex – a Neolithic astronomical observatory?', *Archaeological Journal*, 130: 44–76

Pickles, J. (1985), *Phenomenology, Science and Geography*, Cambridge: Cambridge University Press

Pitt-Rivers, A. (1898), *Excavations on Cranborne Chase IV*, Privately printed

Pitts, M. and Jacobi, R. (1979), 'Some aspects of change in flaked stone industries of the Mesolithic and Neolithic in southern Britain', *Journal of Archaeological Science*, 6: 163–77

Poole, F. (1986), 'The erosion of a sacred landscape: European exploration and cultural ecology among the Bimin-Kuskusmin of Papua New Guinea', in M. Tobias (ed.), *Mountain People*, Oklahoma: University of Oklahoma Press

Price, T. and Brown, J. (eds) (1985), *Prehistoric Hunter–Gatherers: The Emergence of Complexity*, London: Academic Press

RCHM (Royal Commission on Historical Monuments) (1972), *County of Dorset, Vol. IV: North*, London: HMSO

RCHM (1975), *County of Dorset Vol V: East*, London: HMSO

RCHM (1979), *Long Barrows in Hampshire and the Isle of Wight*, London: HMSO

Relph, E. (1976), *Place and Placelessness*, London: Pion

Relph, E. (1981), *Rational Landscapes and Humanistic Geography*, London: Croom Helm

Renfrew, C. (1969), 'Review of "Locational Analysis in Human Geography" by P. Haggett', *Antiquity*, 43: 74–5

Renfrew, C. (1973a), *Before Civilization*, Harmondsworth: Penguin

Renfrew, C. (1973b), 'Monuments, mobilisation and social organization in Neolithic Wessex', in C. Renfrew (ed.), *The Explanation of Culture Change*, London: Duckworth

Ricoeur, P. (1983), *Time and Narrative*, Vol. I, Chicago: Chicago University Press

Riesenfeld, A. (1950), *The Megalithic Culture of Melanesia*, Leiden: E. J. Brill

Roese, H. (1982), 'Some aspects of topographical locations of Neolithic and Bronze Age monuments in Wales', *Bulletin of the Board of Celtic Studies*, 29: 763–75

Ross, M. (1987), 'Kington Magna and surrounding areas: a fieldwalking survey of the prehistory (1979–1987)', *Proceedings of the Dorset Natural History and Archaeology Society*, 109: 91–103

Saville, A. (1990), 'A mesolithic flint assemblage from Hazleton, Gloucestershire, England, and its implications', in C. Bonsall (ed.), *The Mesolithic in Europe*, Edinburgh: John Donald

Savory, H. (1956), 'The excavation of the Pipton long cairn, Brecknockshire', *Archaeologia Cambrensis*, 7–48

Savory, H. (1961), 'Mesolithic site on Craig y Llyn (Glam.)', *Bulletin of the Board of Celtic Studies*, 19: 163–5.

Savory, H. (1980), 'The Neolithic in Wales', in J. Taylor (ed.), *Culture and Environment in Prehistoric Wales*, Oxford: British Archaeological Reports 76

Schieffelin, E. (1976), *The Sorrow of the Lonely and the Burning of the Dancers*, New York: St Martin's Press

Schlee, G. (1992), 'Ritual topography and ecological use: the Gabbra of the Kenyan/Ethiopian borderlands', in E. Croll and D. Parkin (eds), *Bush Base: Forest Farm*, London: Routledge

Seamon, D. (1979), *A Geography of the Lifeworld*, London: Croom Helm

Seamon, D. (1980), 'Body–subject, time–space routines, and place-ballets', in Buttimer and Seamon (eds)

Seamon, D. and Mugerauer, R. (eds) (1989), *Dwelling, Place and Environment*, New York: Columbia University Press

Shanks, M. and Tilley, C. (1982), 'Ideology, symbolic power and ritual communication: a reinterpretation of Neolithic mortuary practices', in I. Hodder (ed.), *Symbolic and Structural Archaeology*, Cambridge: Cambridge University Press

Shanks, M. and Tilley, C. (1987a), *Re-Constructing Archaeology*, Cambridge: Cambridge University Press

Shanks, M. And Tilley, C. (1987b), *Social Theory and Archaeology*, Cambridge: Polity Press

Shanks, M. and Tilley, C. (1989), 'Archaeology into the 1990s', *Norwegian Archaeological Review*, 22: 1–12

Sherratt, A. (1990), 'The genesis of megaliths: monumentality, ethnicity and social complexity in Neolithic north-west Europe, *World Archaeology*, 22: 147–67

Silko, L. (1981), 'Language and literature from a Pueblo indian perspective', in L. Fiedler and H. Baker (eds), *Opening up the Canon*, Baltimore: Johns Hopkins University Press

Smith, A. and Cloutman, E. (1988), 'Reconstruction of Holocene vegetation history in three dimensions at Waun-Fingen-Felen, an upland site in south Wales', *Philosophical Transactions of the Royal Society of London*, Series B, 322: 159–219

Speck, F. (1923), 'Mistassini hunting territories in the Labrador peninsula', *American Anthropologist*, 25: 452–71

Soja, E. (1989), *Postmodern Geographies*, London: Verso

Stanner, W. (1965), 'Religion, totemism and symbolism', in R. Berndt and C. Berndt (eds)

Stanner, W. (1966), *On Aboriginal Religion*, Sydney: Oceania Monograph No. 11

Stanton, Y. (1984), 'The Mesolithic period: early post-glacial hunter–gatherer communities in Glamorgan', in H. Savory (ed.) *Glamorgan County History*, Vol. II, Cardiff: University of Wales Press

Strehlow, T. (1965), 'Culture, social structure, and environment in Aboriginal Central Australia', in R. Berndt and C. Berndt (eds), *Aboriginal Man in Australia*, London: Angus and Robertson

Strehlow, T. (1970), 'Geography and the totemic landscape in central Australia: a functional study', in R. Berndt (ed.), *Australian Aboriginal Anthropology*, Nedlands: University of Western Australia Press

Summers, P. (1941), 'A Mesolithic site near Iwerne Minster, Dorset, *Proceedings of the Prehistoric Society*, 7: 145–6

Taçon, P. (1991), 'The power of stone: symbolic aspects of stone use and tool development in western Arnhem Land, Australia', *Antiquity*, 65: 192–207

Tanner, A. (1979), *Bringing Home Animals*, Newfoundland: Institute of Social and Economic Research

Taun, Y.-F. (1974), *Topophilia*, Englewood Cliffs: Prentice-Hall

Taun, Y.-F. (1975), 'Space and place: humanistic perspective', *Progress in Human Geography*, 6

Taun, Y.-F. (1977), *Space and Place. The Perspective of Experience*, London: Arnold

Taylor, J. (1980), 'Environmental changes in Wales during the Holocene period', in J. Taylor (ed.), *Culture and Environment in Prehistoric Wales*, Oxford: British Archaeological Reports, British Series No. 76

Taylor, L. (1989), 'Seeing the 'inside': Kunwinjku paintings and the symbol of the divided body', in H. Morphy (ed.), *Animals into Art*, London: Unwin-Hyman

Thomas, J. (1991), *Rethinking the Neolithic*, Cambridge: Cambridge University Press

Thorpe, I. (1984), 'Ritual, power and ideology: a reconstruction of earlier Neolithic rituals in Wessex', in Bradley and Gardiner (eds)

Tilley, C. (ed.) (1993), *Interpretative Archaeology*, Oxford: Berg

Tilley, C. (in press), *An Ethnography of the Neolithic*, Cambridge: Cambridge University Press

Turnbull, C. (1961), *The Forest People*, London: Jonathan Cape

Turnbull, C. (1965), *Wayward Servants*, New York: Natural History Press

Turnbull, C. (1983), *The Mbuti Pygmies. Change and Adaptation*, New York: Holt, Rinehart and Winston

Wagstaff, J. (1987a), 'The new archaeology and geography' in J. Wagstaff (ed.)

Wagstaff, J. (ed.) (1987b), *Landscape and Culture. Geographical and Archaeological Perspectives*, Oxford: Blackwell

Wainwright, G. (1959), 'The excavation of a Mesolithic site at Freshwater West, Pembrokeshire', *Bulletin of the Board of Celtic Studies*, 18: 196–205

Wainwright, G. (1963), 'A reinterpretation of the microlithic industries of Wales', *Proceedings of the Prehistoric Society*, 29: 99–132

Watson, P., LeBlanc, S. and Redman, C. (1971), *Explanation in Archaeology*, New York: Columbia University Press

Webley, D. (1959), 'The neolithic colonization of the Brecknockshire Black Mountains', *Bulletin of the Board of Celtic Studies*, 18: 290–4

Webley, D. (1969), 'Aspects of Neolithic and Bronze Age agriculture in South Wales', *Bulletin of the Board of Celtic Studies*, 23: 285–90

Webley, D. (1976), '"How the west was won": prehistoric land use in the southern Marches', in G. Boon and J. Lewis (eds), *Welsh Antiquity*, Cardiff: University of Wales Press

Weiner, J. (1991), *The Empty Place*, Bloomington: Indiana University Press

West, C. (1956), 'Report on the bones from Pipton long cairn', Appendix in Savory

White, L. (1964), 'The world of the Keresan Pueblo Indians', in S. Diamond (ed.), *Primitive Views of the World*, New York: Columbia University Press

Williams, A. (1953), 'Clegyr Boia, St. David's (Pemb.): excavation in 1943', *Archaeologia Cambrensis*, 102: 20–47

Williams, N. (1982), 'A boundary is to cross: observations on Yolngu boundaries and permission', in N. Williams and E. Hunn (eds), *Resource Managers: North American and Australian Hunter–Gatherers*, Boulder, Colorado: Westview Press

Williams, R. (1973), *The Country and the City*, London: Chatto and Windus

Wymer, J. (ed.) (1977), *Gazetteer of Mesolithic Sites*, London: Council for British Archaeology Research Report 22

Zvelebil, M. (ed.) (1986), *Hunters in Transition*, Cambridge: Cambridge University Press

Index

219